Cast Your Shadow: Influence on Purpose

QUIN SHERRER

ISBN-10: 1985098768
ISBN-13: 978-1985098763

DEDICATION

This book is dedicated to four pastors whose shadow fell on me:

Peter Lord, Pastor Emeritus of Park Ave. Baptist Church (part of the Body of Christ) in Titusville, Florida. For six years, after church on Sunday night, eight couples gathered in my home so that Pastor Lord could disciple us. During one year-long study he taught us 35 of the New Testament commands called "One Anothers." Years later I went back to discuss with him those teachings. At age 86 he was still teaching another generation three times a week in his own home.

And to:

The late **Jamie Buckingham**, my writing mentor, author of more than 40 books, a roving editor for *Guideposts Magazine* and the pastor of the Tabernacle Church, in Melbourne, Florida. Jamie's keynote address at an Aglow International Conference some years ago on "Your Shadow Ministry" emanated from his encounter with some new believers from Papua New Guinea on Mt. Sinai. His story jump-started the idea for this book. If someone is indeed "in our shadow," then we are connected to many one anothers. Sometimes deliberately or other times unaware.

And to:

Forrest Mobley, who as rector of St. Andrews Episcopal Church in Destin, Florida, introduced me to the wonderful workings of the Holy Spirit. I was a young mother when I attended his classes during summers while visiting my mom there. He encouraged me to write the first miracle healing in his church which won me a *Guideposts Magazine* writers contest. At the *Guideposts* Writers Workshop in Rye, New York, one of the author-instructors, Jamie Buckingham, who lived less than an hour from me in Florida, agreed to continue coaching me after the workshop ended. Pastor Jamie, in turn, encouraged me to seek out Pastor Peter Lord in the town where I was a newspaper reporter. And the "one anothers" in my life just grew as I allowed their shadows to fall on me. Today Forrest Mobley is affiliated with Immanuel Anglican Church in Destin where I attend since retirement and he is my spiritual advisor and mentor.

And to:

Dutch Sheets, internationally known author, who was my pastor for ten years when we lived in Colorado. While he was writing his now classic book *Intercessory Prayer*, I had the privilege of being one of his intercessors. Dutch opened new doors of opportunity for me to speak across this nation, and I am most grateful for his encouragement and blessing which continues to shadow me.

And to:

Those in the editorial and publishing field who were the guiding lights to get my books into print: Gwen Ellis, Ann Spangler, Don Cooper, Bert Ghezzi, Kyle Duncan, Bill Greigg III, Kim Bangs, Jane Campbell, Jane Hansen Hoyt, and especially to Ruthanne Garlock who co-authored 19 books with me.

Also thanks to:

Fran Ewing and Tommie Woods (both now in heaven) and Beth Alves – all three who pushed me for years to write this book.

A very special thank you to Sherry Grace Anderson and her daughter Désirée Schroeder who made the publication of this book possible. God bless you, dear friends.

And to those who prayed as I wrote:

Quinett, Sherry, Jeanette, Mary Jo, JoNell, Christina, Sally, Kate, Jane, JoAnne, Brenda, Dorothea, Kerry, Lori, Anne, Leslyn, Suzanne, Cindy, Nancy, Martha, Tracey, Charlene, Elizabeth, Wendy, Forrest, Bob, Ken, Mike, Dutch, Dale, and John.

CONTENTS

INTRODUCTION

Live under the protection of God Most High and stay in the shadow of God All-Powerful (Psalm 91:1 CEV).

In the natural a shadow is formed when we get in the sunlight and are illuminated, leaving a darker image of our body's shape. A shadow shows the same image as the silhouette – in this case a person – when looking at it from the light.

In the supernatural God's abiding presence can "overshadow us" and help us cast a shadow on one another by sharing our skills, abilities, knowledge, advice, friendship, or other giftings.

Throughout this book you will find stories of people who influenced or were influenced by another person – shadows were cast. Some you will recognize since they are well known for their contribution to society. Others lived quiet and ordinary lives touching their family, neighbors, church, even strangers. Just "one anothers" whose lives connected and were impacted for good. Some are still letting their shadows fall; still others have gone to their heavenly reward. May you be inspired to reach even more people with your talents and abilities as we review these stories.

I refer to this as our Shadow Ministry, though many of us might hesitate to think we have "a ministry." We just go about our normal day-by-day living and in the process touch and influence others. We experience encounters and connections.

While exploring the Shadow Ministry concept I found many "one another" principles. The words "one another" or "each other" are found 36 to 50 times in the New Testament, depending on which translations you read. Granted, some are what we are "to do" for each other, while others are what "not to do." At least 35 of them are commands! (See Appendix for a list).

I pray that reading testimonies in this book will jump-start ideas for you to share your skills with other "one anothers" to come along and "shadow" you.

Jesus showed the world what love is like and how it acts! God longs to use us everyday folks to make a difference for Him right where we are, as He did. Are we ready? Let's start an exciting journey.

May God show us how and overshadow us as we go. Be blessed.
– Quin Sherrer

******

Look carefully then how you walk! Live purposefully and worthily and accurately […] as wise (sensible, intelligent people) (Ephesians 5:15 AMPC).

Part One

CASTING A SHADOW ON A MOUNTAINTOP

Every good gift and every perfect gift is from above, and comes down from the Father of lights, with whom there is no variation or shadow of turning (James 1:17 NKJV).

"I wonder if so much that we think is insignificant may not be the most important thing in God's eyes. The kingdom of God is carried on the shoulders of people who occupy their shadow ministry." – Jamie Buckingham

God gives us connections. Ponder these questions for a moment. Who is in your shadow? Who are you influencing for God? Whose shadow fell on – or still falls – on you?

God is looking for ordinary people – like you and me – to do extraordinary things for Him. How? By inviting God's abiding presence to "overshadow" and help us make a difference for Him in the lives of those with whom we interact. And in the process influence others.

Who knows when you may discover a result of your shadow ministry – one that will totally surprise you? You go along doing what you always do. Then boom! Someone tells you how your life impacted him, and you had no idea.

It happened to my writing mentor, Jamie Buckingham, author of more than 40 books. He told about his surprise shadow discovery to several thousand women when he was a keynote speaker at the Aglow International Conference in New Orleans several decades ago.

Pastor Jamie often took several men with him on trips to Israel and other Biblical sites, so this was not his first visit. Here in his own words is the story that was tape recorded that day:

I was climbing Mt. Sinai about four years ago, finishing research on a book I was writing. We'd been in the region two weeks and we had finally reached the base and were camping out there. Five men were with me and we were to arise early before dawn in order to be at the peak of the mountain. The mountain is about 7,500 feet tall, a hard, arduous climb. We still had 5,900 feet to go. Pilgrims had climbed this many times in the past.

As we were on our way up before dawn I heard behind me chanting and singing. I looked back and I saw coming up the trail behind me a group of Aborigines – wearing just loin cloths. There were about ten or twelve of them running up the mountain barefoot. They passed me chanting.

I arrived at the top, a little after dawn, and these fellows were all standing around, having their little meeting. I couldn't understand much – they were speaking in tribal language and broken English. The summit of the mountain is a very tiny place, and we were all just sort of crowded in there together.

There was a white man with them. I went over and spoke to him. "What's going on here?" I asked. "Who are all these people?"

"This is the first Aboriginal tribe from New Guinea who has ever left there to come to Israel," he explained. "They wanted to come down to the Sinai Peninsula. They have been sent by their tribe to discover if the places mentioned in the Bible are real or not. There has been a move of God in this tribe in the highlands in Papua New Guinea, and they elected these representatives including the 83-year-old chief who is over there. They worked a year and a half to earn money to come, and other tribes in the area contributed.

"They flew to Tel Aviv, toured Israel, and have now come to the Sinai Peninsula to climb the mountain where Moses received the commandments, to see if there really is such a mountain. They are going to carry this report back with them," he continued.

"That's a remarkable story, but who are you – how did you get connected to them?" I asked.

"I am the missionary. It has been through my ministry that these people have all come to know the Lord. There are 700 to 800 of them in this tribal area who now all know Jesus Christ as Lord," he answered.

"But you are not from New Guinea," I said.

"No, I'm from Australia. I was a biker in Australia, in a motorcycle gang, when I received the Lord. He directed me to go as a missionary to the Aborigines."

"Well, how did you come to know the Lord?"

"I read a book by an American and I received Jesus. You wouldn't know an author by the name of Jamie Buckingham, would you?" he asked me.

"You aren't going to believe what I am about to tell you – I am Jamie Buckingham." There was much rejoicing and handshaking. He took me over to introduce me to these people he'd won to Jesus.

The 83-year-old chief of the tribe who had tattoos across his cheeks, looked up into my face and said, "Thank you for casting your shadow over us." Then again. "Thank you for casting your shadow over us!"

The reference is to Acts 5:12 where the Apostles performed many miracles and were highly regarded. Many people believed in the Lord and laid their sick on beds and mats so that Peter's shadow might fall on them, and all of them were healed.

I had sat down in my office in Florida with my Bible open. In solitude I wrote words. Someone gifted in editing worked on it, passed it on to someone to print it, then someone else gifted in distribution got it. And the shadow went up across the world, ending up in New Guinea.

God says fasten your eyes on Me – ordinary people – and I will do My extraordinary through you."[1]

Author Jamie Buckingham was not alone in spreading his shadow from Florida to Australia and eventually to Papua New Guinea. Those in the publishing field from the first copy editor to the bookstore owner on another continent had a part, each using his or her skill in their routine work day. But what an amazing result. Connected to one another. Influencing people.

Years later I learned that the Speaker of the Papua New Guinea Parliament had called for a National Day of Repentance, and it continued for several years as a national holiday.[2] One year the Prime Minister proclaimed the Word of God as the foundation of the nation. However, even among believers some truths of Christianity are sometimes mixed with traditional tribal beliefs.[3] When I read recently that a large percent of Papua New Guinea citizens identify as Christians, I couldn't help but wonder how many of those men on Mt. Sinai that long ago day had gone home to spread their shadow over their portion of the nation.

Let's think about shadows for a moment. In the natural a shadow is formed when we get in the sunlight and are illuminated, leaving a darker image of our body's shape. A shadow shows the same image as the silhouette, in this case a person, when looking at it from the light. In the supernatural God's abiding presence can "overshadow us" and help us cast a shadow on one another.

We need God's shadow where we have the promise of His presence. "He who dwells in the shelter of the Most High will abide in the shadow of the Almighty." (Psalm 91:1 NASB) Dutch Sheets in his book *Intercessory Prayer* speaks of God's overshadowing:

> "Overshadow is the Greek word *episkiazo* which means to cast a shade upon; to envelope in a haze of brilliancy; to invest with supernatural influence… It is also used in Acts 5:15 when people were trying to get close to Peter – in his shadow – that they might be healed… the Holy Spirit was 'moving' out from Peter – hovering – and when individuals stepped into the cloud or overshadowing, they were healed."[4]

To cast is to "send out, radiate, hurl, fling, give off." When we invite the Lord to overshadow us, we can cast a shadow on those with whom we will have encounters or connections. Let's do it!

Prayer: *Lord, overshadow me with Your presence. Help me in turn to be an influencer for You by casting my shadow over those You choose. I ask in Jesus' name. Amen.*

You Are Him Here

A new command I give you: Love one another. As I have loved you, so you must love one another. By this everyone will know that you are my disciples, if you love one another (John 13:34-35).

"Christ has no hands on earth but yours. No feet on earth but yours, no eyes of compassion on earth but yours. He has no body on earth but yours." – Teresa of Avila, 16th century nun.[5]

The smiling teenager standing on our church's podium that Sunday evening took the microphone. She had been in a juvenile detention home in our town, she explained, but on weekends she had been allowed to visit in homes of our various church families. Now she was going home.

"You fed me, clothed me, loved me and best of all, you introduced me to Jesus. I am so thrilled with what Jesus has done for me, I want to thank Him. But you are Him here, so I will thank you," she said. "*You are Him here...You are Him here*," she repeated over and over, as her index finger pointed out across the audience.[6]

Going home to parents. Going also someday to an eternal home with her heavenly Father. After returning to her hometown she reached out to other girls dealing with temptations like those she had overcome. Influencing others. Shadowing. It has a way of multiplying blessings, one to another.

The week after her goodbye speech, our pastor had dozens of plaques made for those of us who wanted to display one in our home. It read simply "You Are Him Here" as a reminder that we are Christ's representative to anyone who knocks on our door.

Christianity is an intimate relationship with Jesus lived out among one another – believers encouraging and supporting each other with mutual love and concern.

We are indeed His hands, feet, eyes of compassion – here on earth. Each of us has a *shadow ministry*, whether we recognize it or not.

Prayer: *Lord, let me be alert to connect with those whom You choose. I desire for my connections and encounters to be God-ordained. Give me wisdom and discernment needed for what to do when these events happen. Thank You. Amen.*

Influencing with Purpose

"[W]ho has saved us and called us with a holy calling, not according to our works, but according to His own purpose [...]" (2 Timothy 1:9 NASB).

"Our God specializes in working through normal people who believe in a supernatural God who will do His work through them. What He's waiting for is the invitation."[7]
– Bruce Wilkinson

Why is the subtitle of this book *Influence On Purpose*? Sometimes our shadow falls on someone we did not know as with Pastor Buckingham who wrote a book that had a life-changing experience for a biker on another continent. But more often we cast a shadow on purpose on others that influences them, hopefully in a positive way. Let's look at the main meanings of *influencing* and *purpose*.

Influencing: "the power to change or affect someone or something; the power to cause changes without directly forcing them to happen; a person or thing that affects someone or something in an important way." Synonyms include words: prestige, authority, credit, weight. Purpose is "the reason why something is done or used; the aim or intention of something. Other synonyms for purpose: intent, end, goal, design, objective.[8]

I once read that sociologists say we will influence or be influenced by 10,000 people in our lifetime.[9] "Impossible," I said to myself and I still disbelieve it. But think about the "influencers" in our lives: the waiters who have recommended the best lunch choice, the doctor who advised a medical procedure, the teachers and preachers who taught, counseled, and guided us. Add to that employers, co-workers, relatives, neighbors, even strangers like the car mechanic, the plumber, the repairman, the salesmen who have influenced our decisions. Stretch that over the years, and the number grows.

While all of us come under influencers, each of us also influences those with whom we interact, whether in big or small ways through our various encounters! We can then purpose to influence: for good, not bad; to help, not hurt; to serve, not abuse; to encourage, not discourage.

Purpose is a common catchphrase these days used by staff members in churches, businesses, and school systems. Numerous purpose-related workshops and strategies are listed on the Internet. Yet, we must guard against harmful purposes.

Paul advised: "Look carefully then how you walk! Live *purposefully* and worthily and accurately, not as the unwise and witless, but as wise (sensible, intelligent people)" (italics mine, Ephesians 5:15 AMPC).

Rick Warren, whose best seller book *The Purpose Driven Life* helped Americans take another look at how they influence others, gives practical and scriptural principles. He writes:

1. Everybody has influence.
2. God expects me to use the influence He's given me.
3. My influence is for the benefit of others.
4. If I'm not influencing them, they're influencing me.
5. The purpose of influence is to speak up for those that have no influence.
6. I will answer to God for how I used my influence.
7. If I use my influence well, God will give me more.
8. The path to greater influence is service and generosity.
9. You only influence people who trust you.
10. Criticism is the inevitable price of influence.
11. The fastest way to influence is by being likable.
12. Kingdom builders help others use their influence wisely.[10]

"Example is not the main thing in influencing others. It is the only thing," Dr. Albert Schweitzer once said.

Next, we will explore ways we are indeed connected to one another by looking at the lives of some ordinary men and women who were a shadow for others – many as purpose-focused influencers for good.

Prayer: *Lord, thank You that You have a purpose and plan for me. Guide me in it. And help me touch the lives of others for their benefit and Your glory. Amen.*

Think On These Things

Ask God what His purpose is for you individually. Then meditate on these Scriptures as you wait upon Him with the expectation that He will direct you.

- "For everything there is a season, and a time for every matter under heaven" (Ecclesiastes 3:1 ESV). Ask, "Lord what season am I in?"

- "The Lord will fulfill His purpose for me" (Psalm 138:8 ESV). Pray: "I am so grateful, Lord, that You have a specific purpose for me to live out in my lifetime. Help me fulfill it." Job says to God: "I know that You can do all things, and that no purpose of Yours can be thwarted." (Job 42:2 NASB) Pray: "Lord, help believe that Your plan for me will be not be thwarted. Show me how to cooperate with that plan."

Part Two

CONNECTING WITH PURPOSE AND INFLUENCE

Personally, I've been completely satisfied with who you are and what you are doing. You seem to me to be well-motivated and well-instructed, quite capable of guiding and advising one another. So, my dear friends […] I'm simply underlining how very much I [Paul] need your help in carrying out this highly focused assignment God gave me (Romans 15:14, 15 MSG*).*

"Shadowing is simply following someone around who has been serving in an area of interest to you."[1] – Wayne Cordeiro

Deliberate connections happen when we link up with the right people with mutual goals and purposes. Each of us has a specific journey God intends for us to take. The road changes with the various seasons of our lives but He really cares about the people who will walk it with us.

Shadowing, we already know is used in professional circles. A pre-med student shadowing a doctor observes his practice, asks questions, evaluates procedures – just absorbs all he can while following him. He also gains hands-on-training and hopefully a good letter of recommendation later on.

Some companies use "work shadowing" as an on-the-job learning experience. One worker, for instance, may follow a more experienced one for days to weeks to learn a new job or get a better understanding of it. The intent: to transmit knowledge and expertise to one less experienced in that field of work – with purpose, of course. Businesses such as the media, financial institutions, even churches have created internship programs. Some interns get paid; others do not.

How can shadowing be implemented within the Body of Christ? The early church served "one another" or "each other" in what has been called *reciprocal living* as two or more people act equally to one another. (See Appendix.) As already mentioned during the process one's shadow falls on the one who is learning.

The pastor of a large church in Hawaii made an effort to deliberately invite others to come under the shadow of a more experienced church member. In *Doing Church as a Team*, Pastor Wayne Cordeiro explains that part of his church's success came from allowing members to use their talents and gifts, but also by stretching people to do even more. He writes:

"Shadowing is simply following someone around who has been serving in an area of interest to you. It is a way of introducing new people into a ministry, and we recommend this approach in almost every volunteer ministry at New Hope. It's a low-risk orientation that gives budding 'ministers' a glimpse of what is being done and how. It's also an opportunity for everyone to build new friendships along the way.

The three stages of shadowing are:

Stage 1 – I do. You watch.

Stage 2 – We do together.

Stage 3 – You do. I applaud!

Passing the baton is a function of our willingness to allow God to use us fully in ministry. Answering our call and using our gifts includes being led by the Holy Spirit to help others become successful."[2]

The Bible is filled with examples of different abilities. One writer listed these: "artistic ability, architectural ability, administering, baking, boat making, debating, designing, embalming, embroidering, engraving, farming, fishing, gardening, leading, managing, masonry, making music, making weapons, needle work, painting, planting, philosophizing, machinability, inventing, carpentry, sailing, selling, being a soldier, tailoring, teaching, writing literature and poetry."[3] Add to that giving, banking, hospitality, caring for the sick, preaching, writing…and on and on.

Author Bruce Wilkinson says we often think of God's arithmetic for our expanded sphere of influence to look something like this:

My abilities + experience + training

+ my personality and appearance

+ my past + the experience of others

= my assigned territory.

Yet he reminds us God is looking for normal people who will allow Him to work through them and thus His math might look more like this:

My willingness and weakness

+ God's will and supernatural power

=my expanding territory.[4]

Very do-able principles if we keep in mind this Scripture admonition: "Not by might, nor by power, but by my Spirit, says the Lord Almighty" (Zechariah 4:6b). Whether we are the "taught one" or the "teacher one" we do well to depend on God's Spirit to guide and enable us.

Prayer: *Lord, please help me to pass the baton successfully. As I teach others, may I do it unselfishly in gratitude for the abilities You have blessed me with. As I prepare to provide a shadow for someone else please give me patience, wisdom and guidance. Thank you. In Jesus' name. Amen.*

Practicing Shadowing In Practical Ways

Why is it that He gives us these special abilities to do certain things best? It is that God's people will be equipped to do better work for Him, building up the church, the body of Christ, to a position of strength and maturity (Ephesians 4:12 TLB).

"We say we are 'a people built together into a meaningful relationship in Christ.'…It means we are a servant people, freely loving and caring for one another based on the grace we each experienced through Jesus…We strive to be totally committed and totally involved. To expect less is to play church rather than to be the Church."[5] – Karl A. Barden

How can shadowing work within a church body in down-to-earth ways? Suppose you want to learn something practical but you don't have anyone to teach you. Here's one example.

When my children were still young we became active in a church whose pastor truly believed in the New Testament command that each of us should use whatever gifts we have to serve others. The "learner" got under the shadow of the "teacher."

One Sunday, Pastor Peter Lord asked church members who were willing to share their talents to register with the church secretary. Then those who needed help with a project could call to find out who with that ability or experience had volunteered. The intention: hands-on training for practical everyday living!

That's how I found myself one Saturday morning in Margaret's kitchen with my 13-year-old daughter who wanted to learn to bake bread from one of the best bakers in the church. Margaret taught us how to mix, knead, roll, bake.

My experience as a newspaper feature writer prompted me to volunteer to teach a Christian writing class in my home once a month. Over a dozen signed up.

My husband, an aerospace engineer, spent Saturday mornings helping high school and college guys learn how to work on their cars on the floor of our garage.

Elizabeth, owner of a florist shop, taught classes to women on how to create attractive flower arrangements. Each of us got individual attention as we learned to use our creativity to produce beautiful centerpieces for our dining tables.

Jim, who owned a private plane, offered to fly the pastor and his ministering team to out-of-town meetings. My husband volunteered as the extra pilot. While on the trips, Pastor Lord shared practical lessons from his own life with his pilots.

Becky taught young women how to clean house more effectively, using the most efficient and economical cleaning supplies. She'd explain the best techniques for various tasks and then demonstrate.

Gene used his carpentry skills to teach others how to build simple cabinets. James taught young boys and dads how to best catch fish on Fox Lake early Saturday mornings.

Maggie taught good manners classes to the younger girls. Then she showed them how to dress on a lower budget. One-on-one private sessions with the girls occurred after class, sometimes with the moms along too.

Mary Jo enlisted a team of women to makeover homes in our community, from rearranging furniture to making bedspreads, curtains and tablecloths out of decorative sheets. Her crew of women always prayed before "decorating day" began, asking God to help them let each home's décor reflect that family's personality and taste. At last count about 60 women had participated over the years in makeovers in more than 1,000 homes. And they never charged for their services.

And so it went with those who volunteered to help others. Friendships were formed that lasted for years. Young boys grew up to fish and teach their sons on Fox Lake, too.

When we moved to another city I took with me some of Mary Jo's ideas to decorate our home. And Margaret's recipe for making bread. And Becky's spic-and-span ideas for house cleaning. And I praised God for the women from my writing class who sent me copies of their published work, some even years later.

Was this teaching rather than mentoring? Perhaps so. Yet we learned new skills as we often returned to our "mentor-teacher" for follow up advice. Shadowing? Yes!

Reciprocal living affects the total ministry of the church when a deliberate effort is made to implement gifts. Biblical commands are both direct and indirect and specify how Christians are to relate to one another. What they are to do and not do (See Appendix).

The Apostle Peter said: "God has given each of you some special abilities; be sure to use them to help each other, passing onto others God's many kinds of blessings" (1 Peter 4:10 TLB). Pastor Rick Warren tells how his church members use their skills to help others.

"Nearly 7,000 people are using their abilities at Saddleback Church, providing every kind of service you could imagine: repairing donated cars to be given to the needy; finding the best deal for church purchases; landscaping; organizing files; designing art, programs and buildings; providing health care; preparing meals; composing songs; teaching music; writing grant proposals; coaching teams; doing research for sermons or translating them; and hundreds of other specialized tasks. New members are told, 'Whatever you're good at, you should be doing for your church.'"[6]

"Link your gifts with your passion and you will begin to play a powerful role in the Body of Christ. You will find such joy and motivation when this is taking place...and you will experience maximum effectiveness with a minimum of weariness," another pastor suggests.[7]

Yes, God is looking for those of us who have enough passion about our talents we are ready and willing to share. Of course, our individual personalities affect how and where we use those God-given gifts and abilities.

Chuck Pierce sums it up well: we are definitely connected with one another.

"In a society such as ours that places high value on personal achievement it is often hard to understand that our destiny is linked to others. And that we will not succeed alone. We are connected to one another. Therefore, the promise God has for you is incorporated into a greater destiny of which you are a part. Your promise is linked to the overall movement of God, not only in your life, but in your territory, and in the generations past and yet to come. Even though God is a very personal God, He enacts our promises along with those of others to whom He has connected us."[8]

Of course, there are also other reasons for connections. I will never forget the night, sitting out on our screen porch, when Pastor Peter Lord asked if he could use our home to teach seven couples how to walk in victory in our everyday lives. His goal was to link Biblical principles with practical ways to do it. He would teach us on Sunday nights after church and, if we agreed, then on Wednesday nights another 14 people would come to our home for us to teach them what he had taught us. My husband, LeRoy, and I both said "yes." For the next six years, until we moved, we provided the host home.

Our Sunday night meetings started off with fellowship and lively conversations while we enjoyed a light supper. Then Pastor Lord gave us about a 20-minute teaching on our Bible topic with practical illustrations from his experiences. Sometimes his wife Johnnie added her insights. Brief discussions and a prayer time followed. Rather than telling each other our crisis situations, we often prayed them aloud to God while the others added their "amens" of agreement.

The Wednesday night group we led included married couples, single moms, a widow, and a man married to an unbeliever. That meant 16 people in our living room on Sunday nights and another 16 of us on Wednesday nights. Across the city, dozens of similar groups from our church met in homes on Wednesday nights.

Pastor Lord suggested home group guidelines or disciplines to consider for personal, spiritual, physical, and social growth:

- Spending 30 minutes a day in prayer and Bible study, using his book, *The 2959 Plan – A Guide to Communion With God*, as a guide to pray for our families, church, workplaces, city, nation, government leaders and others. For three of those years we fasted every Friday from sunup to suppertime to pray for our nation.

- Praying together with our spouse several times a week, if married. Otherwise, get a prayer partner who could keep confidences.

- Keeping our family high on our priority list.

- Praying at the church's Prayer Chapel at least 30 minutes during the week.

- Being hospitable to someone for Christ's sake sometime during each week (sharing a meal at work, home, or even a picnic).

- Keeping our body or "temple" fit by exercising at least four times during the week.

- Keeping fresh in our minds how to give a personal testimony in a short time span.

Not long ago I went back to visit that church and talk with some of the people who had met in our home groups. I personally thanked Pastor Lord for equipping us more fully for day-to-day dependence on the Lord, regardless of our circumstances. He was one of the greatest influencers in my life. As I write this, he is still teaching small groups – but this time as a widower in his own home. The sign outside it reads: "Welcome to the Lord's house."

The Apostle Paul wrote: "And there are distinctive varieties of operation [of working to accomplish things] but it is the same God Who inspires and energizes them all in all" (1 Corinthians 12:6 AMPC).

So, let's get on with what He has called us to do. Now, rather than later. Cooperating with Him as He directs and orchestrates. Connecting. Influencing.

Prayer: *Lord, help me to be more willing to teach and help others. Show me what, where and how to accomplish what You want done! Thank you or the talents You have put in me and may I use them to bless others more fully. Bring the right people into my life to help me do what You intend for me to accomplish. I thank You in advance. Amen.*

Think On These Things

When I asked a few friends what they think it takes to be a good influencer, they made these comments:

- Be interested in others. (When you meet them for first time, write their name in your smart phone to help you remember it and call them by name from now on.)

- Learn to be a good listener. (Listen intentionally to what they say.)

- Guard what you say. (It is better to say nothing than to criticize.)

- Treat them with respect and consideration, just like you would like to be treated.

- Remember, you are influencing others every day, for good or bad, so try to be positive, not negative in your talk and actions.

- If asked to share your wisdom or talents, do so if you feel "right" about doing it, but set your own timetable. (Pray first to determine if this is a genuine hands-on-connection for you.)

- If you decide to mentor/influence others in a closer relationship, guard yourself from trying to control them and find better ways to offer them helpful direction.

Part Three

MENTORING ONE ANOTHER

And let us consider and give attentive, continuous care to watching over one another, studying how we may stir up (stimulate and incite) to love and helpful deeds and noble activities (Hebrews 10:24 AMPC).

"I'd rather see a sermon than hear one any day
I would rather one would walk with me than merely show the way...
The lectures you deliver may be wise and true
But I'd rather get my lesson by observing what you do."[1]
– Edgar A. Guest

Observing what you do! Being mentored. What is mentoring exactly? "A mentor is someone further down the road from you who is willing to hold the light to help you get there."[2] "Shadowing" jumps out at us in that definition. A mentor lets you fall under his shadow as he holds the light to guide you.

Mentoring has been described as the "passing down of knowledge, on a one-on-one personal relationship as one shares from his or her life experience." It says, "I want to see you succeed." Here is an example.

For over fifty years, Howard G. Hendricks was a beloved professor at Dallas Theological Seminary. During his lifetime he authored books, spoke in over 80 countries, served as chaplain to the Dallas Cowboys football team, and was a keynote speaker for The Promise Keepers and other well-known groups. Even in his eighties he was still travelling to minister. Today pastors are preaching to thousands via television and in stadiums while others are reaching congregations in cities and small hamlets around the world because of his influence.[3]

But who was the encourager for this future seminary professor destined to touch thousands? In his book *Mentoring*, Bobb Biehl lets Dr. Howard Hendricks tell his own story of how he was born into a broken home in Philadelphia and nobody cared about his spiritual life. Then a small group of believers started an evangelical church in his neighborhood. One man named Walt, who wanted to teach Sunday School, was told to go gather some boys from the neighborhood and that would be his class. Dr. Hendricks tells it:

> Walt came out. I'll never forget the day I met him. He was six feet, four inches tall. He said to me, as a little kid, "Hey, son, how would you like to go to Sunday School?" Well, anything that had 'school' in it had to be a bad news item! And then he said, "How would you like to play marbles?"

Oh! That was different! Would you believe we got down and played marbles, till he beat me in every single game. I lost my marbles early in life. And by the time he got through, I didn't care where he was going; that's where I wanted to go.

He picked up thirteen of us boys, nine of us from broken homes… Today, all thirteen of us are in full-time vocational Christian work. And Walt never went beyond sixth grade… I am moving today because of a man who not only led me to Christ, and discipled me, but started that mentoring process."[4]

Who knows the number of students who were mentored and encouraged while Walt taught them? Dr. Hendricks himself said mentoring is "a ministry of multiplication" and a "biblically legitimate strategy for our generation."[5]

Author Bobb Biehl suggests this exercise for seeing how the mentoring process could multiply: Pause for sixty seconds and try to imagine the implications of this:

You mentor 12, who mentor 12, equals 144!
Who mentor 12, equals 1,728
Who mentor 12, equals 20,736
Who mentor 12, equals 248,832
Who mentor 12, equals 2,985,984.[6]

Now if that sounds staggering, try mentoring just one or two.

Prayer: *Father, thank You for those who are willing to share their skills and experience in a mentoring setting. Let me be open to mentor even a young person who needs my encouragement, not counting the cost in time, wisdom and patience it will require. Help me, Lord. Amen.*

Pass It On

Pattern yourselves after me [follow my example], as I imitate and follow Christ (the Messiah) (1 Corinthians 11:1 AMPC).

Follow God's example, therefore, as dearly loved children and walk in the way of love, just as Christ loved us… (Ephesians 5:1-2).

"I will look for opportunities to encourage others to bring out the best in them and to help them accomplish their dreams. I will speak words of faith and victory, affirming them, approving them, letting them know they are valued…helping them to rise higher and become all that God created them to be."[7] – Joel Osteen

You have probably heard the saying, "If no one is following you, you are just taking a walk." Is someone replicating your life? Imitating you?

Paul wrote the Philippians, "The things which you learned and received and heard and saw in me, these do" (4:9 NKJV). "Model your way of living on it," (4:9 AMPC). To the Corinthians: "Imitate me, just as I also imitate Christ." (1 Corinthians 11:1 NKJV)

What did he mean when he said, "imitate me"? Probably this: "when I invest my life in others, imitate me." Let's take a closer look:

Imitate what you have learned from me

Imitate what you have received from me

Imitate what you have heard from me

Imitate what you have seen in me

Imitate me as I imitate Christ

Practice those things!

Do those things!

Model your way of living on it.

To the Thessalonians Paul wrote: "For you yourselves know how you ought to follow our example" (2 Thessalonians 3:7). The Greek word for "follow" here means *"mimic"* or "actor." It implies to study the life, deeds, actions of a person to duplicate or reproduce those attributes that you observe in their lives.

Toward the end of her life, here's how one grandmother passed on similar advice. Her son was none other than the world-famous evangelist, Dr. Billy Graham.

Gigi Graham, eldest of the five children of Billy and Ruth Graham, became the mother of seven and grandmother of more than a dozen. In her book *Passing It On*, she writes about the last visit she and her children and grandchildren had with their beloved grandmother "Mother Graham" in her red brick farmhouse.

Gigi said her grandmother looked so small and frail sitting on the edge of her bed, yet she was full of joy and happiness to see them. As they approached her bedside, the elderly woman enfolded each in her feeble arms and gave him or her an explicit verse or blessing. Then with deep conviction she said, "Pass it on."

A few days later Mother Graham died. But she left a spiritual heritage to several succeeding generations – one that Gigi was sure will bring strength and joy to her children and their children and their children.[8]

Bobby Conner said it so well: "Just as every human on earth has distinct fingerprints, so also each of us has a unique legacy. Legacy can be likened to the footprints of life. Just as footprints in soft sand reveal that someone has passed this way, so too your legacy is evidence that you were here on earth, and it points to your accomplishments. Legacy is the fragrance of your life, which lingers long after you have departed from the room."[9] One author wrote:

> "Have you had a kindness shown? Pass it on.
>
> 'T'was not given for thee alone, Pass it on.
>
> Let it travel down the years,
>
> Till in heaven the deed appears
>
> – Pass it on."[10] – Henry Burton (1840-1930)

Think now of a special "pass it on" legacy that was left you. How about one you want to leave?

In the book *And the Good News Is… Lessons and Advice from the Bright Side*, Dana Perino tells how she and some acquaintances came up with the idea of mentoring aspiring young women who are starting their professional careers by offering fast-paced sessions called "Minute Mentoring."

Dana, who had served for over seven years in the administration of President George W. Bush, kept getting requests from young rising professional women wanting advice on how best to achieve their life and career goals. So "Minute Mentoring" was born, a take-off on speed dating, but in leadership skills, not romance.

Here's how it works: women leaders from various professional fields meet personally in a seminar type setting but with small groups of mentorees to share their top three pieces of advice, and then take questions during the allotted time. That group later moves to the next mentor. Usually the mentorees hear six mentors, and finally they attend a reception where the women practice their networking skills. (Later even some young men asked to participate.)[11]

Dana likes to help young professionals think through what they need to improve their careers but she also teaches them some hallmarks of becoming a good leader. Those who are mentored are encouraged to pass on what they have learned. The Internet lists many mentoring programs.[12]

We all know leaders who were developed through the mentoring process. John Maxwell, one of America's experts on leadership, teaches a five-step process to train people. He used these successfully in his San Diego church and has taught them to thousands through seminars and books. He advises, "Don't equip people who are merely interested, equip the ones who are committed."

Maxwell uses "I" to explain the steps he, which are summarized here.

- I model the tasks while the person watches.

- I mentor, continuing to do the task while the person I am training comes alongside me to assist. I explain the how and why of each step.

- I monitor as the trainee performs the task and I assist and correct.

- I motivate and let the trainee go, encouraging him and staying with him until he senses success.

- I multiply – when the trainee has done the job well, it is his turn to teach others how to do it. The best way to learn something is to teach something, he advises.[13]

Mentoring then can be done in a fast-paced manner as Dana's "Minute Mentoring," or over a longer time span when teaching a trainee. But both methods encourage the one taught to teach someone else. It's an admirable goal.

As I write this from my east coast home I am mentoring a 50-something grandmother from California via e-mail and she in turn mentors a younger woman once a week in Kentucky via phone, as well as several younger women in her area. I meet too with a younger woman every other week while we sit at a picnic table after our nature walk. She takes notes to pass on what she is learning to a group of three she mentors. Multiplication results.

Yes, let's go equip those who are committed.

Prayer: *Father, You who are our Friend and full of surprises, we thank You for opportunities to glean from one another during our life's journey. These are precious times, and we do not take them lightly but with a heart of gratitude.*

Lord, thank you for all the creative ways You have ordained that we can learn from others. We thank You in advance for bringing the right resources and people into our lives to better equip us for Your plan. I ask in Jesus' name. Amen.

Spiritual Moms Needed

Likewise, teach the older women to be reverent in the way they live… to teach what is good. Then they can train the younger women to love their husbands and children, to be self-controlled and pure, to be busy at home, to be kind, and to be subject to their husbands, so that no one will malign the word of God (Titus 2:3-5).

"A happy homemaker, convinced of her importance as an individual and a contributor to the lives of those around her, forms the backbone of the family. And in turn, good families constitute the building blocks of society. Women in the home, therefore, can exert a crucial influence on their society." – Baukje Doormenbal[14]

Numerous young mothers long to be nurtured, accepted, encouraged, and to be held accountable to an older woman. They want to grow and become all God wants them to be. Mary Jo Looney was a spiritual mom to many in her church, including me. But Renee, a mother of six wrote me a letter once about what Mary Jo had meant to her.

For twelve years Mary Jo served Renee breakfast at her house on Tuesday mornings. Some days Renee took her children along; other days her mother-in-law kept them. She wrote me:

"God brought Mary Jo into my life when my third child was just a baby and I desperately needed the encouragement of an older woman. She has been to me 'Jesus with skin on.' When I would arrive at her doorstep tired and weary from the demands of motherhood, she provided refreshment to my body, soul, and spirit. She helped me to focus on God's value system and what is really important in life. She always urged me to remember that each child is God's righteous seed to raise for His glory. I have become a better mother and wife as a result of her godly influence."[15]

Some years ago God impressed on Mary Jo to open her home on a regular basis for young women to come to be taught and encouraged. It was not uncommon for two dozen young women to gather once a month so that she and several other older women could mentor them. Before they'd leave they met in smaller groups to pray for one another. Some who came were new in the community in need of a friend. Others had emotional or spiritual needs and knew they could receive prayer.

Some told her they enjoyed giggling when they discovered they were "normal." New moms brought their babies soon after birth for the others to see, love and pray over. It went on year after year. These women did not want a pal, they had their friends. They wanted a role model, a resource person, someone to answer their questions, challenge and even correct them. They looked to Mary Jo and her older friends to help them become all God wanted them to be. And they wanted to meet on a regular basis to keep growing.

Even in her golden years, Mary Jo was still teaching young women in her home as they sat at her feet listening to her homespun humor and Biblical truths. They desired to be a better disciple of Christ's – yet have fun on the King's highway of life. Shadowing I've discovered, is often the best way to implement "one anothering."

Ideally when you enter a mentoring relationship to encourage others, it is wise to have a mutual understanding from the start. When mentoring four single gals from my church once a month at my house, I first asked what they wanted to accomplish. "To learn homemaking skills before we marry," they said. So that's what we concentrated on.

I set some ground rules. They needed to be committed to attending our meetings and to do their homework assignments. Occasionally a few other women came to help teach in areas where I did not have as much expertise. One evening I had the young ladies prepare a meal in my kitchen and serve it like I had taught them. They had to make a centerpiece, set the flatware properly, cook and serve the meal (serve guests on the left, remove plates from the right). At the end of the year I felt they were well equipped and we no longer needed to meet. To our delight, one soon married.

A word of caution though. Sometime along your mentoring journey you may experience disappointments if those you are trying to help reject your guidance. They may fail you, misunderstand you, or decide to quit.

Jesus' disciples fell asleep in the Garden of Gethsemane before His arrest and He had been their teacher/encourager/mentor for three years. His inner circle of disciples, Peter, James, and John, misunderstood His mission on the Mount of Transfiguration; one even wanted to build three tabernacles and just stay. After Jesus' death Peter said, "I'm going fishing." But look how God used all three of those mighty men later.

Be discerning about the one you agree to mentor because it is going to cost you time and personal sacrifice. A church staff member I know agreed to mentor a college student one summer because the girl's parents asked. The church even paid her while she interned for 15 hours a week. However, it was not to be a good fit, possibly due to the student's lack of interest.

If the person you are mentoring seems disinterested, talk to her about it, and seek God on whether you are to let go and mentor someone else. But don't quit praying for the drop-out. Ask God to bless her and to fulfill His destiny for her. The day may come when what you tried to impart returns to her remembrance to help her.

Please don't be afraid to mentor out of your own trials as well as your triumphs. If you are a woman who has ever had a miscarriage, been caretaker for an elderly parent, been a single mom, had a husband delivered from pornography, moved around a lot – if you came through to victory, you probably have the right know-how to mentor another woman to wholeness (with God's wisdom and guidance, of course). No doubt you have a lot of empathy and compassion to understand a situation akin to what you have walked through. So be willing to pass it on. I agree with this writer about God using us:

"You are not too young, too old, too damaged, or too late to be used of God. God does not need the best, the brightest, or even those who might seem the obvious choice – what He needs is people with a great big "yes" in their hearts." Let's say "YES" to those He sends into our lives and help them grow."[16]

We agree. Yes, Lord, here we are.

Prayer: *Thank You, Lord, for those with creative abilities who have taught and encouraged me with their talent. Bless them for the time and energy they spent on my behalf. Please reward them in ways that I can't. Thank You, too, for those who have allowed me to mentor them and who are even now mentoring others. Your glorious network system is amazing, Father God. Thank You, again. Amen.*

Think On These Things

Some general mentoring guidelines I used over the years are listed here. Of course, not every one of these suggestions fit every mentor/mentoree relationship. Naturally, you would adjust them to fit your unique situation and goals and come up with your own.

- Decide when and how often you will get together. Weekly or monthly? Or if not in person via phone or e-mail?

- Be committed to a schedule and ask for a commitment for a set time.

- Discuss your goals for mentoring. What does the one you are to mentor want to gain from your time and advice? What do you think is an attainable goal on your part?

- Will you mentor one-on-one or meet with several people at a time?

- Decide which study guides, workbooks or Bible portions you will explore together. Or if you just want to meet and ask questions.

- Pray daily for the person(s) you are mentoring but also ask her to get a prayer partner.

- Encourage her to keep some type of journal noting what she is learning and what God is showing her.

- Teach her in such a way that she/he can teach others.

- Remember that your hopes are that your disciple will take your ideas and build on them, going even beyond you, the mentor.[17]

- Caution: don't become emotionally dependent on one another. Don't let the relationship become so consuming you neglect your own family and close friends.

Biblical Mentoring Examples

You may want to study some of these mentoring examples in the Bible. While our circumstances are certainly not the same as theirs, the choices they made and the results they experienced may prove just the lesson God has been trying to whisper to us for our own lives. Examples of biblical mentoring:

Elijah and Elisha: 1 Kings 19:19-21; 2 Kings 2:1-15.

Moses and Joshua: Exodus 17:9-14; Deuteronomy 31:14, 23; 34:9.

Ruth and Naomi: Ruth 1:16-22; 2:11-22; all of chapters 3, 4.

Mary and Elizabeth: Luke 1:39-56.

Paul and Barnabas: Acts 9:1-27; 11:22-30; 13:1, 2, 7, 42-50; Acts 14:1-7.

Paul and Timothy: 1 Timothy 1:1-5, 18; 2 Timothy 2:1-13; 3:14-17; 4:1-9, 23.

Jesus and disciples: All four Gospels and especially the books of Luke and Mark.

Aquila and Priscilla and Apollos: Acts 18:24-28; 1 Corinthians 3:4-7.

Part Four

ENCOURAGING ONE ANOTHER

Therefore, encourage one another and build each other up, just as you are doing (1 Thessalonians 5:11).

"Barnabas was the kind of person who saw something of great value and worth in another person and did everything he could to promote that person – he promoted Paul's ministry instead of his own."

– James W. Goll

Think about it. Where would you be today without someone significant in your life who encouraged you? Prayed for you? Gave you money? Offered a shoulder to cry on? Made you laugh? Gave you a job break? Ran interference for you? Led you to Christ?

There are probably a lot of somebodies who encouraged you along your journey. In today's vernacular "encourage" can mean to cheer, inspire, boost, reassure, give confidence, help turn someone from discouragement.

New Testament believers were told to encourage each other daily (Hebrews 3:13). The Biblical command "to encourage" has several shades of meaning: *build up, to urge forward, advise, comfort, console, exhort, entreat, counsel.* To encourage: The prefix *en-* means "to make, or put in." When coupled with the word *courage,* it literally means "to create courage or to put courage inside someone." Sometimes *exhort* and *encourage* are used interchangeably. Exhort is a strong word: to spur, push, press, urge, prod.

Barnabas, whose name means "son of encouragement" was perhaps the Apostle's Paul's chief encourager. You know the story: Saul, a former persecutor of Christians, experiences the living Christ on the road to Damascus while en route to harm believers. After his supernatural encounter with the Lord, he becomes an ardent follower of Jesus and preaches fearlessly in His name. Even his name is changed to Paul. (See Acts 9:17.)

But how will the apostles know Paul's transformation is genuine? His reputation as one who hunts down Christians to have them killed is well known. How can they trust him? Will spiritual jealousy engulf them since he claims to have met Jesus?

Enter Barnabas. He finds Paul, takes him to the apostles in Jerusalem and verifies his story. Paul is then accepted and goes on to be one of the greatest evangelists and teachers of the early church. Have you ever considered that Paul might not have fulfilled his call if it were not for Barnabas fulfilling his?

We later see Barnabas ministering in Antioch, where believers were first called Christians. There, he "…began to encourage them all with resolute heart to be true to the Lord; for he was a good man, and full of the Holy Spirit and of faith. And considerable numbers were brought to the Lord. And he left for Tarsus to look for Saul" (Luke 11:23b, 24, 25 NASB). Here we see Barnabas continuing his mission of encouragement wherever he went.

Let's look at another New Testament example. Apollos, a Jewish Christian who preached boldly in the Ephesus synagogue, was known as "a learned man, with a thorough knowledge of the Scriptures, who spoke with great fervor and taught about Jesus accurately, though he knew only the baptism of John" (Acts 18:25).

Along came two encouragers. Priscilla and Aquila, who after hearing him speak, took him aside to explain more accurately to him "the way of the Lord." Obviously he was a willing pupil. They taught, exhorted and encouraged him to grow even more in his knowledge and faith. He was built up and urged forward. (See Acts 18:24-26.)

A short time later when Apollos wants to go to Achaia, "the brothers encourage him and write to the disciples there to welcome him. On arriving, he is a great help to those who by grace have believed" (Acts 18:27). Once encouraged, Apollos encourages others. The shadow lengthens.

All of us can build up one another no matter where we are in our Christian growth. Ultimately we express Christ's love as we do.

Prayer: *Father, thank You for Biblical examples of encouragers. Help me to be one in my sphere of influence. In Jesus' name I ask this. Amen.*

Sister of Encouragement

[He whose gift is] practical service, let him give himself to serving [...] He who exhorts (encourages) to his exhortation; he who contributes, let him do it in simplicity and liberality; he who gives aid and superintends, with zeal and singleness of mind; he who does acts of mercy, with genuine cheerfulness and joyful eagerness (Romans 12:7a, 8 AMPC).

"Mutually caring relationships require kindness and patience, tolerance, optimism, joy in other's achievements, confidence in oneself, and the ability to give without undue thought of gain. We need to accept the fact that it's not in the power of any human being to provide all the things all the time."[1] – Fred Rogers (*Mister Rogers' Neighborhood*, Television Hall of Fame)

How can we encourage someone daily? Words – spoken and written – are powerful tools for encouragement. Two of my friends illustrates this.

They lived 500 miles apart but for some years they prayed on the phone together daily for each other and their families. Once a year they got together when Julia's family vacationed near Sarah. Then Julia got sick. Twice cancer went into remission as they prayed and then rejoiced over the phone together. A few years later it returned and affected her swallowing and speech. The doctors told her it was terminal.

When praying for ways to encourage her friend, Sarah decided to write her a letter or a card every single day. She included Scriptures and specific incidents of what their friendship meant. She wrote how she admired her as a great friend, wife, mom and grandmother and expressed thanks for ways Julia had impacted her life by her prayers, humor and advice.

Tears ran down Julia's cheeks whenever her daughter read the letters – piled on Julia's bedside table – to her over and over. For three months the letters came daily. Until that March afternoon when Julia slipped into the arms of Jesus.

Sarah told me: "Julia had invested in my life for years by praying with me. I wanted to encourage her by letting her know she had blessed and influenced many lives. She was main intercessor for her pastor and church, and over a span of twenty years she had mentored countless young women there. As Julia's influence spread over many of us, we are richer spiritually."

You can probably think of many reasons why we need to encourage each other. A few include:

- When we are discouraged over day-to-day situations.
- When we want to move toward new goals, fulfill dreams.
- When experiencing a serious health issue.
- When we are weary in well doing.
- When temptations lure us toward sin.
- When jobs/home/family are in a crisis mode.
- When financial setbacks plague us.

- When health issues seem overpowering.

- When going through a divorce. Or a death in the family. Or making a move to a new town.

- When we need help to do a seemingly impossible task.

Ask yourself, "What can I do to be an encourager?" Offer a listening ear? Be a hands-on helper in a difficult situation? Give when financially able? Make a phone call? Be a Barnabas, a Priscilla or Aquila?

Prayer: *Lord, help me become a better encourager – to cheer someone on to be all You created him or her to be. Spotlight to me those who You want me to encourage right now. Then give me courage and strength to do so. Amen.*

A Surprise Encounter

Jesus Christ is the same yesterday and today and forever (Hebrews 13:8).

"Every experience God gives us, every person he puts in our lives, is the perfect preparation for the future that only He can see." – Corrie ten Boom

Divine encounters. Chance meetings. Sometimes a "someone" crosses your path just once in your lifetime but the encounter is so startling you smile years later remembering it.

After boarding a plane in Colorado Springs headed to Virginia to do a television interview on a new book I'd written, I carefully studied passengers as they boarded. You could spot the military men even those in civilian clothes by their particular haircuts. They differed from the Olympic athletes, vacationers, and business people who passed down the aisle.

When we got off in Chicago to make connecting flights, I was surprised to see a young man about the age of my adult son who had been on my plane, waiting for me.

"Lady," he said, "We have a mutual friend."

"Well, who is it?" I asked puzzled. "You look military."

"Yes, I am but my friend is not. He is the Jewish Carpenter from Nazareth."

"How do you know I know Him?"

"I watched you on the plane – reading your Bible," he explained.

"Yes, and I am on my way to talk about Him on a television show but I may miss my plane since we are running late."

He asked where I was headed, checked the overhead monitors, grabbed my carry-on bag and yelled, "Follow me, I'll get you there." We made a mad dash on escalators, down long corridors. I ran almost every step to keep up with him.

Just as we arrived at my gate, the airline attendant announced last call for passengers to board. My soldier boy handed me my luggage. I waved good-bye. But I forgot to tell him about the sign in my writing office: My Boss Is A Jewish Carpenter.

Whenever I see that sign – still there after many years and moves – I think of the young man whose shadow fell on me that autumn morning. At the right place at the right time with a serving heart. My airport angel. He may have headed off to war after September 11,

2001 events. But someday we'll meet in heaven with our very famous "Mutual Friend." Our Savior, Jesus Christ.[2]

Right now think about an encouraging coincidental meeting you have had, a God-inspired encounter, perhaps with someone you didn't even know. Make you want to laugh aloud? Or fall on your face in thanksgiving to the Lord?

Prayer: *Thank You, Father, for encouraging us through encounters with some people with whom our lives have connected, but are often unplanned. When these amazing events happen, I am surprised but most grateful. I praise You for such serendipities in my life. Amen.*

Do Not Lose Heart

Let us not lose heart [...] for in due time we will reap if we do not grow weary (Galatians 6:9 NASB).

"Make every present moment count."– Anonymous

I was shocked to my core when a biopsy revealed that I had a cancerous tumor. Following surgery, the oncologist recommended 33 radiation treatments as "a good preventive choice." So, I agreed. In the meantime, I was most concerned about side-effects, especially radiation burns as I had seen on my mother during her ordeal.

After finishing the eighth of my treatments I checked my website when I got home. A man wrote that I had sat next to him on a plane years ago, adding, "You were a wonderful inspiration to me. Would you take a call?" As we talked on the phone later he explained that he had been in medical school at the time of our airplane encounter over 20 years earlier.

When he said he was now a doctor, I shared about my ongoing radiation treatments. Shortly afterwards he sent me a wonderful surprise, a box of special cream to apply before and after radiation treatments to help prevent burns.

I smiled in amazement at this timing and connection. "God already knew I'd need to know this future doctor when I grew older and He arranged our meeting long ago for my benefit, for my encouragement," I thought to myself.

One evening I jotted in my journal two sentences I'd heard a television preacher say: "When you feel discouraged or weary in the fight, declare to your situation what you know to be true about God. Speak just one word of encouragement and hope."

Then some days later while facing radiation, I reread the words, deciding to put them into practice. I could be "a word encourager" by speaking God's word aloud. During my early morning 15-mile drive to the clinic I listened to hymns to help me focus on God. Then sitting in the parking lot I'd ask Him for a specific word for that day for me and for others I'd meet.

Minutes later, dressed in my pink gown and just before entering the radiation room, I'd say to the three therapists, "The word for today is…" followed by just one word. Hope. Trust. Courage. Comfort. Wisdom. Strength. One particularly rough day it was three words: "Be not anxious." Some days even before I spoke, a therapist would ask, "What's our word today?" One morning she said, "I needed that." Sometimes a waiting patient would ask me also for "the word." On my final day, I shouted JOY as I rang the celebration bell.

Two months later when I returned for my follow up exam, one of the therapists ran up to me, "I really miss hearing your word for today," she said. "Do you have one now?" And I did. While I originally thought the word was mainly to encourage me, it turned out to also encourage others. God's like that – He spreads encouragement around.

My friend Maria's husband, Brady, suffers from dementia. Before she goes to work, she stops by his nursing residence every morning to have coffee with him. Each evening she eats supper with him there and helps settle him in bed. Then she plants a big kiss on his forehead. She hopes that the next morning when he looks in the bathroom mirror and sees her bright red lip print on his forehead, he will somehow know she had been with him and she will be back today. He has been hers for almost 45 years. So, she marks him with her kiss of love each night.

God marks His children, too. He knows those who are His. Even in our desperate days or nights, He's there with us. His mark is not visible like the red lipstick, but it is there nonetheless. (See Ezekiel 9:4-6.) God's desire is for us to be His instrument of hope and encouragement.

Can we be a somebody to someone who needs encouragement today? Maybe even speak just a word?

Prayer: *Lord, I am thankful You never leave or forsake Your children. Thank You that You send people into our lives to encourage us, but You also allow us to* *be encouragers to others. Lord, help me always be ready to speak Your word of encouragement and hope — because that is what Jesus did for me. Amen.*

Think on These Things

- Think of incidents when someone encouraged you. Make a list and then thank God for each who met your need.

- Think of ways you can be an encourager this week. Write a letter? Send a card? Make a phone call? Treat to lunch? Help them move? Pray for them? Drive someone to the doctor's office? Offer to read to a shut-in? Listen to a discouraged friend?

- Now read Joshua chapters one and two. Joshua, Moses' successor to lead the children of Israel into the Promised Land, is encouraged by God Himself to be strong and courageous. Ponder this verse: "Have I not commanded you? Be strong and courageous! Do not tremble or be dismayed, for the Lord your God is with you wherever you go" (Joshua 1:9 NASB). Think of ways you can use this verse or this Bible story to encourage yourself and others? One important take-away is that the Lord promises to be with us wherever we go.

Part Five

CONTRIBUTING TO NEEDS OF OTHERS

Be devoted to one another in brotherly love [...] contributing to the needs of the saints, practicing hospitality (Romans 12:10a, 13 NASB).

"Whatever our gifts, education, or vocation might be, our calling is to do God's work on earth. If you want, you can call it living out your faith for others. You can call it ministry. You can call it every Christian's day job. But whatever you call it, God is looking for people who want to do more of it."[1] – Bruce Wilkinson

Unique. Creative. One-of-a-kind. God's looking for His children who are willing to stir up the gifts He's given them to reach others, no matter how insignificant we think they are. Let me share about some people who did just that. They cast their shadow. The first never even met those who felt her influence.

Mae, a Texas grandmother with a very limited income, was taking a class on finding your niche in life, but was unable to define hers. Driving home after class one night she was crying because she did not know what her ministry could be. Then she prayed aloud: "Lord, isn't there something I can do without pay that would help others and please You? Show me, show me."

When she walked into her living room, He clearly said, "Here it is." Hanging on racks were children's clothes that had been there for two years. She and a friend had made them but did not know how to market handmade things, so they stored them there.

As she stared at the little dresses, she remembered a newsletter she had read two weeks earlier in a ministry where she works. The director for an orphanage in India had written asking for Christians to come and shower love on the 21 children there. Since she could not quit her job and go for even a short-term mission, she dismissed the plea.

But now, at this moment, God pulled one sentence from the letter and brought it to her heart. "The children came here with nothing but the clothes on their backs." Now she saw it – their clothes were on her racks. She did have a mission. After all, she had been sewing since she was a child, and at one time had even once designed costumes for dinner theatres in New York.

Another memory flashed across her mind. When she was eight years old and not living with her parents, someone gave her a new Christmas dress with thirty-five tiny buttons on it. Every time she wore it she felt special, knowing someone cared enough to touch her life. She could do that for orphans way across the ocean. She could make them clothes.

She decided to call her small ministry simply "Mrs. Buttons" and not only would she make them clothes, but on the inside of every outfit, she would sew a little button in a hidden place with instructions for the child to find it. Whenever they saw or felt the button they would know that someone in America was praying for them.

"Who would have thought God would use me, my ability to make clothes, and even use tiny buttons to reach children halfway around the world? I'd found my niche," she told me.

Though I have lost contact with her, when we talked last, Mae was still making clothes for the little girls. She bought T-shirts and shorts for the boys, but they too got a special button sewn into their clothes. Three women eventually helped sew on buttons while others helped her buy boys' outfits. Her volunteer helpers also prayed for the children. Twenty-one orphans in India came under Mae's giant shadow all the way from Texas, as recipients of God's love shared in such a practical way.

Mae and her friends were obeying the commands: pray for one another, encourage one another, bear one another's burdens. I have wondered how many of those children, most grown by now, went on to cast their shadows on others.[2]

You don't need to have a "big" ministry for your shadow to fall on others. What counts is that you are serving out of heart of compassion as the Lord inspires you in specific ways. My friend Ruthie chose a simple way.

She started renting a small apartment in the South each winter not only to stay warmer but to be nearer her grandchildren. But how, she wondered, could she reach those in her apartment complex where she was known as "the winter snowbird."

She began placing Christian books and tracts in the communal laundry room. Many residents who were of varied nationalities and religions, waited there while their clothes washed and dried. Some of the women just might read what she put out – if only to practice reading in English. Whenever one of the inspirational paperbacks disappeared, she'd buy another to replace it.

Before long when some of the women discovered she was the person supplying the laundromat with books, they'd start a conversation with her. Once in a while a woman in a broken English accent would ask Ruthie to pray for her. I told her once, "Ruthie, you will never know until you get to heaven how many lives you have touched. I know you bathe those women in prayer while you are there."

Maybe hers is not what others call a "stand-out ministry" but in God's eyes, she has been a light in a needed place – and a shadow fell.

Prayer: *Heavenly Father, please show me my special niche; show me simple ways that I too can serve those You want me to reach. Then give me the courage and boldness to do it. I ask this in the name of my Savior, Jesus. Thank You so much. Amen.*

Looking Beyond Ourselves

If your gift is [...] giving, then give generously; if it is to lead, do it diligently; if it is to show mercy, do it cheerfully (Romans 12:6-8).

"We all need someone to believe in us. To see the best in us and to help bring it forth! Sure, we may have many faults that still need to be corrected, but what we need are people who will look beyond our glitches and see God's best."[3]
– Wayne Cordeiro

Grandma Lucy found an unusual way to reach her neighborhood. The oldest resident in the trailer park, she lived in a faded mobile home, in a city known for its hot and humid climate. My friend Kathy, who met her, wrote this:

Most would consider it an unbearable place to live, considering the roar of motorcycles, loud music, numerous verbal disputes, exhaust fumes from the nearby highway and the smell of garbage in the dumpsters. The police came through regularly.

Lucy did without air-conditioning to save money. But she had a plan to touch her neighbors. Before the hot sun rose, she got up early in the mornings to bake cinnamon rolls.

Passerby smelled the mouth-watering fragrance. Lucy went to her door and invited them in. Certain ones came each day. She'd offer some homespun wisdom along with a hot cinnamon roll and a few words of encouragement for their day. Over time and in a natural way, she introduced her new friends to Jesus, her Savior.[4]

A little widow living on social security in an undesirable neighborhood made a difference in the lives of numerous people who came to her door simply because she used her gift of hospitality. I've often wondered how many came under her shadow. Or how many came to know the Lord because of her loving outreach to them? Eternity holds the answer.

God indeed specializes in working through people who allow Him work through them. Did someone like Grandma Lucy ever affect your life?

Prayer: *Lord, help me to remain so much in Your shadow that others who come under mine will feel Your presence and be touched for Your kingdom. Amen.*

Thanking Others

I thank my God upon every remembrance of you, always in every prayer of mine making request for you all with joy (Philippians 1:3, 4 NKJV).

"Do all the good you can, by all the means you can, in all the ways you can, in all the places you can, to all the people you can, as long as you ever can." – John Wesley

God can speak to us anyway He chooses – as He did to me when just one paragraph in the newspaper grabbed my attention. An advice columnist published a letter from a successful artist who said when she had attended her fiftieth class reunion, she learned that her high school art teacher was still alive. She wrote a letter to that teacher, thanking her for her encouragement to her as a student, and explained how art had greatly enriched her life.

The teacher answered back, saying she was aware of this student's success, but in all the years she had taught this was the first pupil to write and thank her.

The Lord pierced my heart. How many people had I written to thank over the years who had made a difference in my life? To my mentors? Friends? Spiritual moms? Pastors? Bosses? I sat down that afternoon and wrote five letters of thanks to let some Very Important People in my life know how powerfully they had impacted me by something they had said or done or given to me.

One of those who had graciously shed his shadow on me was Bob, the editor of the local newspaper where I worked as a feature-writer part time for eight years. In our growing community many residents were somehow linked to nearby Kennedy Space Center and at the time it was one of the closest newspapers of its size covering cutting edge events.

I thanked him for opportunities to interview and photograph many notables who attended space launches while we watched from bleachers as the vehicles lifted off from the launch pad. I mentioned humorous events like the time our city celebrated its 100-year anniversary and we rode on a newspaper-sponsored parade float dressed in period costumes. He looked handsome sporting a specially grown goatee while I struggled with my bulky old-fashioned outfit.

Then I got a reply. In his shaky handwritten thank-you note he told me he was so touched by my long "remembrance epistle" that he had shared it with a few others. Not long afterwards, following a fall at age 90, he left this earth. In the years since he edited me, I shared some of his editorial tips in classes I taught, and more than a dozen of those students have now published their books. So Bob's shadow has lengthened.

I am so glad I answered the nudge to write him. But how many others have I neglected to thank?

Is there someone you need to thank? Recognize? Find? Ask God and He can direct you. He can speak to you even through the most unusual ways. We may chuckle when we read that God used a donkey to speak to Balaam in the Old Testament account. But He can use people, nature, animals or any other means to direct our attention to what He wants done.

Prayer: *Lord, forgive me for procrastinating and failing to let others know how much they have impacted my life. Don't let me be in such a hurry that I fail to say thank-you to those who have allowed their expertise to enrich my life. May You Yourself, dear Lord, reward those who let me walk under their shadow. In Jesus' name. Amen.*

Feeding the Homeless

Then the righteous will answer him, "Lord, when did we see you hungry and feed you, or thirsty and give you something to drink? When did we see you a stranger and invite you in, or needing clothes and clothe you? When did we see you sick or in prison and go to visit you?" The King will reply, "Truly I tell you, whatever you did for one of the least of these brothers or sisters of mine, you did for me" (Matthew 25:37-40).

"When I see a deed of kindness, I am eager to be kind."
– Edgar A. Guest

A shadow of blessing fell on some fortunate folk when a sad situation was turned into a happy event for them one October evening. A wedding was called off but a reception for over 100 people was already paid for at one of Sacramento's finest hotels.

The mother of the intended bride made a surprising decision. "When I found out that the wedding would not be taking place, it just seemed like, of course, this would be something we could give back," she told a television station reporter.

The non-refundable wedding flowers were sent to a local nursing home. Homeless shelters were asked to invite their residents to the wedding feast. So approximately 90 homeless came to the hotel – families, singles, even grandparents. They dined on appetizers, salad, gnocchi, and salmon, among other foods. Some even dressed up for the lavish dinner.

The mother of the intended bride greeted guests. "Even though my husband and I were feeling very sad for our daughter, it was heartwarming to see so many people be there and enjoy a meal," she said.

One woman who attended with her husband and five children expressed gratitude: "To lose out on something so important to yourself and then give it to someone else is really giving, really kind." Her husband added, "It's a blessing."[5]

Thousands heard about those blessed by the Sacramento wedding reception because the story was spread throughout the media. And the host's kindness was not easily forgotten. Jesus saved the day at a wedding reception when He turned water into wine. No one forgot that wedding! We even talk about it today.

Now think a minute. Don't you know someone who contributed to the needs of others – yet it was never publicized? Maybe it was for you. Thank God for it. Maybe it was a compassionate act you did. Relive the joy. Do another. And another.

Prayer: *Lord, thank You for those with unselfish motives who sow kind deeds – turning what could be sorrow into joy for others. Give me creative ways to do this, too, to contribute to the needs of others by finding ways to bless them. Amen.*

Think On These Things

Maybe you want to spend some time contemplating questions about your own involvement in meeting needs of others.

- Are there people you have meant to help but your busyness has kept you from contacting them?
- Are you ready to make a decision and set a goal about doing something? Even setting a time limit?

- Think of ways you can extend hospitality, even if you are on a limited budget. (Take a picnic lunch to work to share with a co-worker?)

- When the simple act of kindness (or a big one) is finally accomplished, hear the Lord's words of pleasure, "Well done, good and faithful servant."

Part Six

PRAYING FOR ONE ANOTHER

[P]ray for one another [...]. The effective prayer of a righteous man can accomplish much (James 5:16 NASB).

"Talking to men for God is a great thing, but talking to God for men is greater still."– E.M. Bounds

H ave you considered how big a shadow you can cast doing something that won't cost you a dime but will require precious time? The answer: prayer. And the rewards can be eternal.

Look around and you may see an opportunity in an unexpected situation, as we become Jesus' representative among our family, neighborhood, community or wherever He chooses. My friend had such an opening with a stranger while grocery shopping.

Twice Barbara caught herself staring at a young woman, an extremely attractive, petite blond – a total stranger. She thought,

"Lord, You have such good taste to create someone so beautiful. But she is troubled. Please touch her hurt."

Standing in the check-out line, Barbara told the woman that God drew her attention to her. Tears gathered in the woman's eyes. Barbara asked, "Could we talk after we've paid for our groceries?" "Yes, of course." As soon as they were seated in Barbara's car, she asked the woman, "Do you know the Lord?"

"I used to," she said, "and when you said God drew me to your attention, I knew He hadn't forgotten me." She told Barbara she was about to be married but that day doctors had told her she had cervical cancer – the test results from her premarital exams.

Barbara, a woman of great faith, prayer and boldness, asked if she could pray for her complete healing. She nodded in agreement. Barbara prayed, asking the Lord to heal her body and soul. They exchanged names and phone numbers.

Two weeks later the young woman called with good news. She was cancer free. As the two of them had prayed in Barbara's car that afternoon, she'd received a physical healing – and an emotional one too. She went ahead with her wedding plans. She made a recommitment to the Lord and continued to get teaching and prayer when she attended Christian women meetings with Barbara for some months afterward.[1]

A chance encounter in a supermarket? No, I think it was a divine setup. Barbara, in the right place at the right time, was sensitive to His Spirit to reach out to a young woman in a tender place, who was ready to respond to His wooing. A beautiful healing resulted.

Dutch Sheets, in his classic book *Intercessory Prayer*, challenges us with our choices:

> There are many wounded and hurting individuals around the world. You work with some, others live across the street. One of them probably just served you in a check-out line, seated you in a restaurant or served you food. Their chains are alcohol, drugs, abuse, broken dreams, rejection, money, lust…
>
> Plan A is for supernatural, but ordinary people like you and me to (1) wholeheartedly believe in the victory of Calvary…and (2) to rise up in our role as sent ones, ambassadors, authorized representatives of the Victor. Our challenge is not so much to liberate as to believe in the Liberator – to heal as to believe in the Healer.
>
> Plan B is to waste the Cross; to leave the tormented in their torment; to scream with our silence: "There is no hope"; to hear the Father say again, "I looked but found no one.[2]

Another friend used a workplace opportunity to encourage a patient. When Trina, a pregnant woman struggling with bouts of vomiting and dehydration, checked into the hospital in an attempt to avoid miscarrying her third child, Dawn was assigned to help her get settled in the room and begin her treatments.

While unpacking Trina's suitcase, Dawn pulled out a paperback version of the Bible titled *The Book* and put it on the bedside table. "That's my favorite book, too," she said with a smile.

"It used to be my favorite," Trina answered glumly.

"Well, maybe God's giving you some time to spend with Him while you're in here for rest and recuperation," Can I pray for you?" Dawn asked.

"Okay," Trina agreed.

Dawn prayed for healing for the mother and the baby – especially that Trina would have enough strength to carry it to full term. "Lord, make Yourself known to Trina in a powerful way during these next few days," she finished.

Dawn's nursing shift changed, and patient and nurse didn't see each other again. Six years later, Trina attended a women's conference where I was teaching on prayer. Dawn had come as my prayer partner and I asked her to lead a worship chorus to open the meeting.

After the session was over, Trina rushed up to Dawn. "I recognized your voice when you began to sing today. You are the nurse who prayed for me to carry my baby full term. Today we have a healthy, beautiful 6-year-old daughter," she said.[3]

Tina went on to tell Dawn that while still in the hospital she turned her life over to the Lord, completely. She also began to pray persistently for her husband, a professional musician who played rock-and-roll music in bars and clubs. He started going to church with her, and a man he met there agreed to mentor him. Her husband was now a musician at their church, and they had plans to open a facility to help young women in crisis situations.

Dawn had spent just a few minutes with a patient in a hospital room where she worked, yet she cast a shadow on Trina's life, which expanded to her husband and their family. A happenstance encounter between the two women at our conference? I don't think so. I believe once in a while God gives us a peek at how He used us in ways we did not yet know. Just to encourage us!

We all have a "little world" of people around us for whom we can pray.

Prayer: *Father, thank You for directing our steps and enabling us to say just the right words to help accomplish what You want said to those in our path. Keep us sensitive to the Holy Spirit's leading so we can be Your ambassadors wherever we go. Amen.*

Praying for Families

For God so greatly loved and dearly prized the world that He [even] gave up His only begotten (unique) Son, so that whoever believes in (trusts in, clings to, relies on) Him shall not perish (come to destruction, be lost) but have eternal (everlasting) life (John 3:16 AMPC).

"Whenever God determines to do a great work, He first sets His people to pray." – Charles H. Spurgeon

Jackie turned 91 just hours before she died. Sitting in the chapel that warm fall morning waiting for her funeral service to begin, I pulled from my memory bank a time frame I considered her biggest shadow-casting moment. Here is how it happened.

One summer some decades earlier, I had gotten a call along with other friends in her church circle, asking us to begin to pray earnestly for her to influence her family for Christ. It was time to attend her family reunion up North again and she usually got a lot of hateful teasing and name calling since she had become a Christian and abandoned her New Age beliefs. But she had planted a lot of prayers for them.

She made it through most of the week with her extremely large family of siblings, aunts, uncles, and cousins. With the exception of one sister, she was perhaps the only Christian. As they casually sat around outdoors visiting one afternoon, a sister stood and said, "These reunions are such fun I think we should continue them someday in heaven. But we all better be sure we know how to get there. Jackie would you come tell us how so we can attend another family reunion in heaven?"

At first Jackie was shocked, but thrilled that she was asked to share the gospel. She rose from her chair and stood beside her sister in front of the crowd.

"Well, praying for salvation is special, but it is not just so we can go to heaven. It is special for here on earth, too. Jesus came to give us life abundant. Salvation includes other things," she said as she continued explaining. Then she asked them all to repeat a prayer after her.

"Father, I come to You, admitting I need Jesus as my Savior. I ask for Your forgiveness for my sins, for your mercy, peace and direction in my life. I am sorry for ways I've disappointed You. Thank you that Jesus died for my sins, I receive Him now." She continued leading them in a prayer to surrender their wills to His will and purpose.

Forty of her relatives came to the Lord that day! Her long-time prayers for those lost but beloved relatives were answered suddenly on an ordinary afternoon. And we who had stood in the prayer gap with her rejoiced when she got home and phoned with the good news![3]

Prayer: *Father, thank You for sending Jesus to die for our transgressions. Thank you for bringing our loved ones into Your Kingdom and that we will someday have that reunion in heaven with them. Amen.*

Praying For Children of All Ages

Know therefore that the LORD your God, He is God, the faithful God, who keeps His covenant and His lovingkindness to a thousandth generation with those who love Him and keep His commandments (Deuteronomy 7:9, 10 NASB).

"Children. To me the very word sparkles with life and laughter! From babies to teenagers, children teem with energy. And each one of them represents a life of potential – for our Lord and for mankind. Nothing demands that we lean on the Lord more than parenting."[4] – Elizabeth George

All children need prayer – the godly and the wayward, the young and the adult, the healthy and those with special needs, the adopted and the stepchild, the unborn and the chronically ill. There is no greater demonstration of God's power to our children than when they see their parents receive answers to prayer. Let me tell share an example.

Some years ago a group of five women in Lexington, Kentucky read my first book on *How to Pray for Your Children* and went on a weekend retreat to watch the accompanying video. Afterward, they decided to meet regularly to pray for one another's youngsters, numbering about 30 children and grandchildren.

"We saw a need to build a wall of prayer around our children because the enemy was seeking to destroy some of them," Elizabeth, the leader, told me later. At first the women met in parks. Then they shared their vision in local churches, home groups and schools. And "Pray for Your Children" groups spread.

Before long, the husbands of the original five women asked if they could pray corporately with their wives. Gathering at Dorothea and Bob's home one night a week, the group, which now included some single parents, started off with fellowship and a covered dish supper. Reports of answered prayer were shared, then the larger group broke up into smaller prayer circles to pray for each other's children. Finally, each person took the names of children other than their own to pray for during the following week.

Twenty years later, the original group was still involved in this prayer effort. I often visited with them at Dorothea's and Bob's home, and left excited and encouraged by their faithfulness. The last time I was in Lexington, a pastor had asked me to come teach a new generation of younger parents how to pray for their children.

After I had finished the seminar, four young women came to introduce themselves. "We want you to know that we are the fruit of our parent's prayers. They were in some of those early Pray For Your Children groups and we knew they were praying for us. Thank you for coming to help them back then," one told me. I put my arms about them and we prayed. My silent prayer was: "Lord, bless these and their generation and raise up parents who are willing to pray for their children, no matter what their circumstances or ages."[5] (See my book, *A Mother's Guide to Praying For Your Children*.)

Have you considered praying with other parents for both your children and theirs? Ask Him for some creative ways to do that. But remember confidentiality is an important rule when sharing about youngsters.

Prayer: *Lord, thank You for caring parents who pray specifically for their children daily, standing in the prayer-gap for them through victories and challenges that try to hinder Your plan for them. May the Holy Spirit guide them in their prayer-time. Help them to trust and lean on You. In Jesus' name. Amen.*

Praying With One Accord

With all prayer and petition pray at all times in the Spirit, and with this in view, be on the alert with all perseverance and petition for all the saints (Ephesians 6:18 NASB).

"Prayer is a powerful thing, for God has bound and tied Himself thereto. None can believe how powerful prayer is, and what it is able to effect, but those who have learned by experience." – Martin Luther

Not only do we want to partner with God when we pray – being in alignment with His will – but as we've already mentioned, having a prayer partner or prayer support team is a powerful source of strength. Jesus Himself said, "Again, truly I tell you that if two of you on earth agree about anything they ask for, it will be done for them by My Father in heaven. For where two or three gather in My name, there am I with them." (Matthew 18:19, 20) To agree here means to pray together in harmony much like a symphony orchestra.

When the 120 were in the Upper Room waiting for outpouring of the Holy Spirit, they "all continued with one accord in prayer and supplication" (Acts 1:14a KJV). The word accord means "being in agreement, having group unity, having one mind and purpose."

Can people praying in one accord impact a whole city? Yes, yes, yes! It happened during World War II in the small community of Seadrift, Texas located on the Gulf Coast. Here's the account as I wrote about it in *Lord, I Need To Pray With Power*:

At the suggestion of a local pastor, a group of wives, mothers and men met at the First Assembly of God Church every morning at 10 a.m. to pray for the safety of the servicemen from their community. Members brought photos of each soldier and made a huge framed collage of the men – 52 in all.

This picture provided a prayer focus point. One mother had five sons in the war. Imagine how she felt when she looked at the large picture of men in uniform and prayed for her precious boys among them.

After the war was over in 1945, every single serviceman came home alive from whatever theater of war he had served in.

Fifty years later, in 1995, I watched a television program on the 700 Club where some of these intercessors and several servicemen – all elderly now –were interviewed. Naturally, it touched my heart.

One woman said, "We didn't just pray at ten in the morning. We prayed night and day for those men." Another intercessor commented, "We stood on the 91st Psalm, reading it every time we met. We prayed at the church. We prayed at home. It seemed like we had that burden and it just stayed with us."

Several of the men who had served their country commented: "All the people in the city here prayed. If somebody had not prayed for us, I don't think a lot of us would have made it back…We knew God was going to take care of us with our mothers and everybody here at the church praying…We knew that we were in the hands of God."

Some of the former servicemen gave testimonies of their narrow escapes in combat and how they knew they were spared because God answered the faithful prayers of those dedicated intercessors.[6]

The united wall of support from folks in Seadrift demonstrates how prayer partners from various walks of life can gather to pray in unity with a mutual purpose and faith that God answers prayers. Seadrift stands out as an example of a community joined in prayer that cast a big shadow over 52 men stationed around the world.

The power of continuous prayer is a precursor to great and mighty things God wants to accomplish.

Prayer: *Father, God, Savior, I thank You for answering prayer. When we read stories of how You touched individuals, families, and communities, our faith rises to a new level. We praise You for You are trustworthy and faithful. Thank You, Lord. Amen.*

100-Year Prayer Movement

The fire must be kept burning on the altar continuously; it must not go out (Leviticus 6:13).

"The Moravians decided to accept the task of keeping a continual fire of prayer, intercession, and worship burning before the Lord's presence…Their motto in the 1700s was 'To win for the Lamb the rewards of His suffering.'"[7]

– James Goll

One of the most amazing prayer movements in history occurred within the Moravian community of Herrnhut – located on the southeastern border of Germany across from Poland and the Czech Republic. In 1727, an around-the-clock "prayer watch" began and continued non-stop for over a hundred years.

But during its first few years of existence, the Herrnhut settlement showed few signs of spiritual maturity. In the beginning the community of about three hundred people was wracked by dissension, bickering, and judgmental attitudes. Yet they committed to get their hearts right and continued to pray for revival. On May 12, 1727 when all discord ceased, revival came and unbelievers were converted.

Count Zinzendorf, who had been the group's leader at age 27, remembered the exact day and the four glorious months that followed their breakthrough revival: "The place represented truly a visible habitation of God among men," he wrote. "A sense of the nearness of Christ bestowed, in a single moment, upon all the members that were present; and it was so unanimous that two members, at work twenty miles away, unaware that the meeting was being held, became at the same time, deeply conscious of the same blessing."

At first a total of 48 women and 48 men signed up to pray – men together, women together, for one hour watches until the next team relieved them. And so it went, "hourly intercession" to be continued by their descendants after them for those 100 years. By

1792, some 65 years after start of the original prayer vigil, the small Moravian community had sent 300 missionaries around the world.[8]

During the Great Awakening in England and America in the eighteenth century, thousands were swept into God's Kingdom because of Moravians. John Wesley, an Anglican minister, was one of them. He had met some Moravians on ship returning to England after conducting what he considered a dismal evangelic ministry effort in Georgia. Their prayer life greatly touched him. especially on the ship returning to England when a fierce storm raged and most feared for their life but the group of praying Moravians.

Once back in England, at a low point in his life, Wesley reluctantly attended a group meeting in a Moravian chapel on Aldersgate Street in London the evening of May 24, 1738. While someone was reading from Martin Luther's "Preface to the Epistle to the Romans" Wesley said his heart was "strangely warmed." In his journal he wrote: "I felt I did trust in Christ, Christ alone, for salvation; and an assurance was given me that he had taken away my sins, even mine, and saved me from the law of sin and death."

He so aligned himself with the Moravian society that in the next year (1738) he went to study at Herrnhut, the Moravian headquarters. While he and his brother Charles established the Methodist movement, the date of John Wesley's Aldersgate experience in a Moravian chapel is still celebrated in Methodist churches on May 24. A big shadow that continues to fall began in a prayer movement in Germany![9]

My friend James Goll, who has made an in-depth study of the Moravian Watch, even travelling there to pray, comments:

"Your prayers can make a vital difference, especially when you harmonize in prayer with others and carefully target your prayers. Since prayer is unhindered by time, distance, or language barriers, you can join any ministry team on earth…Your prayers actually can influence world leaders and activate the resources of God."[10]

We dare not dismiss the impact of the giant shadow that spread – because a prayer watch that ascended unceasingly to the Lord for those many years. God can do it again. And we can be involved in such a movement.

Prayer: *Father, thank You that You are always there to hear our cry for the lost to be saved and for Your glory to be revealed on earth – as it is in heaven. Show Yourself strong on behalf of our nation. Forgive our sins of omission and commission. Help us reconcile to our brothers and sisters in Christ. We thank You for sending Jesus to die for our sins and for preparing a place for us when we leave this earth. Help me to be ever alert to pray as You desire. Amen.*

Standing for Our Neighborhood and City

Our Father which art in heaven, Hallowed be Thy name. Thy kingdom come, Thy will be done in earth, as it is in heaven (Matthew 6:9b, 10 KJV).

"We are to petition our heavenly Father…to approach Him with bold confidence knowing He is our Friend and Father. We ask according to His will (1 John 5:14), not to try to wrestle something He might not want to give. We are laborers together with Him (see 2 Corinthians 6:1)."[11]

– Dutch Sheets

God wants us to pray for the peace, prosperity and welfare in the region where we live. (See Jeremiah 29:7 in several translations.)

One summer several churches in our city joined in agreement to pray for blessings on our neighbors this way: Five blessings for – Five neighbors for – Five minutes a day – Five days a week for – Five weeks. Our pastor even suggested some might want to pray for five co-workers in their "work neighborhood."

Those of us who agreed to ask God to bless our neighbors were given some suggested helps. One I took to heart was to use the word "bless" as a prayer springboard as we prayed over our neighborhood:

B Body: health, protection, strength

L Labor: work, income, security

E Emotions: joy, peace, hope

S Social: love, marriage, family, friends

S Spiritual: salvation, faith, grace[12]

My husband and I saw some amazing results as we prayed together for our neighbors those five weeks. In fact, one woman we didn't even know knocked on our door to ask for help in a crisis situation.

We were able to explain the gospel to several of her family members as a result.

Through the years I have had some rewarding experiences praying one-on-one, as well as being a part of small prayer groups. For seventeen years, every weekday at 8:00 a.m. I prayed on the phone with my friend Lib for five minutes. Since we had seven youngsters between us, our children were our prayer focus.

Later when my family moved, I learned that a woman named Fran Ewing, who attended the church we joined, had been led to the Lord by the Dutch evangelist Corrie ten Boom. Now, I wanted Fran to teach me to pray as Corrie had taught her.

Corrie's family and friends, working with the Underground in Holland, had helped save over 800 Jews from being killed by the Nazis. Betrayed by a fellow countryman, she and other family members were sent to Nazi death camps. Her elderly father and beloved sister Betsy died in prison. Due to a clerical error, Corrie was released the week that women her age were to be killed. After World War II, Corrie travelled the globe sharing her love for the Lord and her lessons on forgiveness. Many came to hear her simply because she was a Holocaust Survivor. Her life was depicted in the widely acclaimed book, *The Hiding Place* by John and Elizabeth Sherrill, and the movie by the same name.

But over a period of 16 years, Corrie wrote some of her smaller books while staying in her special bedroom in the home of Fran and Mike Ewing, in three different states where they had lived. I had met Corrie when my writing mentor Jamie Buckingham was ghostwriting her *Tramp for The Lord* book which detailed her evangelistic speaking travels around the world. In the 33 years after the war she travelled to 60 nations, sharing about Jesus.

When I asked Fran if we could be prayer partners, she agreed but said there were three other women she wanted to include. She offered us her home at 5:30 on Monday mornings for one hour.

For the next three years we met in her living room to pray for our families. After the other women left to get husbands off to work, Fran and I spent the next hour visiting over breakfast. Her husband Mike, a paraplegic due to polio, was still asleep. Often I pelted Fran with questions about Corrie, or prayer, or whatever concerned me. Sitting in rocking chairs on her spacious front porch she had helped me brain storm on the first book I wrote, *How to Pray for Your Children*.

We continued to pray together after our prayer circle disbanded. And after my husband and I moved away, we prayed together on the phone. But a dozen years before Fran's death, we returned "home" to Florida and once again we met for prayer sessions. She was on dialysis the last six years of her life – three days a week for four to five hours, hooked up to machines – and she withstood many scary hospital trips for other health issues.

Whenever I visited her during her last months, I plopped down in a chair beside her bed, read to her for a while, and then handed her the hymnbook. She would sing some of the great old hymns in her beautiful soprano voice as we worshipped together. Often I asked her to sing those she had sung at my mother's funeral and both of us shed tears. My mother and Corrie had died just a few days apart.

One day after Thanksgiving, Fran called me on her cell phone while undergoing dialysis at the hospital. "Call the pray-ers. I am having a hard time breathing," she said. Twenty minutes later she was face-to-face with her Savior whom she so dearly loved. How I treasure the times I spent with Fran, Lib, Dee, Tommie, and my other prayer partners over the years.

Today when time seems short, relationships hard to find, and privacy prized, we must not allow excuses to prevent us from wanting, seeking or finding the right prayer partners.

Nowadays my other prayer partners and I connect with one another by texting, e-mails, mobile phones and in person when possible. (See my book *Lord, I Need to Pray with Power.*) But I have one friend who lives in another state who prays with me via phone every weekday morning for two things: our families and our nation.

During my early morning devotional time with the Lord, I have some "helps" in my bedroom to aid me.

- Prayer chair: a special chair I sit in while I pray.
- Prayer journal: to record my daily prayers for my family, friends, nation.
- Bible with notes.
- World map: often I study the world map when praying for a certain country.
- List of governmental officials: to pray for them by name.

- Prayer board of photos: this corkboard is covered with pictures of those that I pray for on a regular basis. Many live in other states. They vary from business men and women to missionaries, to close friends and of course family members. Some are young, some are in their golden years. Some of them are committed to pray for me, too.

Prayer Board

For those on my prayer board, I ask God that they will experience what I call "the five Ps." I ask for them to know God's: Presence. Protection. Provision. Peace. Precious promises to be fulfilled. Next, I pray specifically for various situations I may know about. It may include for them to:

- Have discernment and wisdom and not be deceived in decisions facing them.
- Make wise choices financially and morally.
- Have favor in the marketplace.
- Cast their cares, worries, anxieties on the Lord, trusting Him.
- Have the right people come into their life at the right time.
- Have a positive influence as they use their talents and skills to help others.
- Experience God's healing/comforting touch to those who need it.[13]

Recognizing our extended sphere of influence, we can see what a privilege it is to come boldly to the throne of God on behalf of others. One great way is to pray the Lord's Prayer for them, beginning with "Father, Your will be done in their lives – on earth as it is in heaven." (See Matthew 6:9-13.) In His model prayer, Jesus gave His disciples guidelines: "lead us not, but deliver us" as though He was expecting them to pray together.

Prayer: *Lord, thank You for the friendships that are closer knit when we pray for one another. Thank You, too, for the opportunity to pray for those we may never meet, just because You give us a "prayer burden" for them. What a privilege prayer is. Amen.*

Think On These Things

Prayer partnerships should consist of those who can pray with shared concerns and similar goals. We can ask the Lord to lead us to the right prayer partner or support team, trusting His timing and recognizing He wants to be included in any prayer partnership.

Consider Prayer Partner/Group Guidelines

- Decide on a specific time to meet for prayer and commit to it.
- Set a time limit.
- Know your focus/purpose for prayer. Don't get sidetracked with other topics.
- Maintain confidentiality, humility, and forgiveness.
- Guard against judgment and unforgiveness.

- Don't hog all the allotted time; give others an opportunity to pray.

- Be accountable: speak the truth to each other without fear of rejection.

- If you do not agree with a prayer offered, tell the others why.

- Agree to pray during the week for each other.

- A time may come when you can no longer meet with the group, because of time limits or other obligations, so be honest enough to drop-out and not delay their meeting.

Praying Scriptures for the Lost

The Word says: "The Lord is not slow about His promise, as some count slowness, but is patient toward you, not wishing for any to perish but for all to come to repentance" (2 Peter 3:9 NASB).

I pray that "God will grant them repentance leading them to a knowledge of the truth, and that they will come to their senses and escape from the trap of the devil, who has taken them captive to do his will" (2 Timothy 2:25b, 26).

I pray that God would "open their eyes so that they may turn from darkness to light and from the dominion of Satan to God, in order that they may receive [...] an inheritance among those who have been sanctified by faith in Me [Christ]" (Acts 26:18 NASB).

When Praying For Others

- Be specific. See Luke 11:5-13. He asked specifically for three loaves of bread.

- Be persistent (Luke 11:5-9). Keep asking, seeking, knocking. The three imperatives are in the Greek present tense: denoting a continuous asking, seeking, and knocking.

- Learn faith-building Scriptures to use in a crisis and overcome fear.

- Ask God for Scripture promises and cling to those for your loved ones, believing that God is faithful.

- Pray for God to send Christians across the path of your loved ones to talk to them about the things of God.

- Get a prayer support team to stand with you.

- Hold onto your faith that with God, nothing is impossible (no one is hopeless).

- Personalize scripture for your situation.

- Don't be a worry "pray-er." Jesus said, "Be not anxious." Live in faith, not fear.

- Don't dwell on all the negatives – the things in the natural that are wrong but pray believing that God has the answer on the way.

- Don't box God in by your own expectation and timetable. We may be tempted to tell Him how we want our prayers answered and when, but remember He knows best and His ways are higher than our ways. Be open to the Holy Spirit.

Part Seven

SERVING ONE ANOTHER

Each of you should use whatever gift you have received to serve others, as faithful stewards of God's grace in its various forms. […] If anyone serves, they should do so with the strength God provides, so that in all things God may be praised through Jesus Christ (1 Peter 4:10a, 11a).

"Take that gift God has entrusted to you, and use it in the service of Christ and your fellowmen. He will make it glow and shine like the very stars of heaven." – John Sutherland Bonnell

Jesus, knowing who He was, where He had come from, and where He was going, took a towel and washed His disciples' feet as they gathered for the last meal He would have with them before His crucifixion. By taking the role of a servant, Jesus gave us an example to follow, though we may find other ways to serve one another.

Here is such a story of a man who had a servant's heart even after he gained notoriety. His name is Eric Liddell (1902-1945).

In Paris that Friday evening, July 11, 1924 the crowd in the Olympic stadium roars with excitement as Eric Liddell, the runner from Scotland, crosses the finish line winning the 400 meter race – setting a new world record of 47.6 seconds. No one gave him a chance at winning a gold medal. He is shortest of the six runners, running on the track's outside lane, and he trained for the 200 meters race. Anyway, an American is expected to win.

Eric finds himself in the peculiar 400 meters competition because of his conviction to honor the Sabbath, refusing to run the 200 meters scheduled for Sunday. Instead, he goes to church. Newspapers chide him because he refuses to run in the race he had practiced for. But just before he is about to race for the longer one, a man slips a piece of paper into his hands with these words. "Them that honor Me will I honor" (1 Samuel 2:30).

Eric Liddell's incredible race was documented years later in the movie "Chariots of Fire," winning the Academy Award for best picture in 1981. In the movie his sister discourages him from racing. She believes he will abandon his plan to return to his boyhood home of China as a missionary, where their parents are still serving. He assures her he will go but he tells her he believes God finds pleasure in his running.

He wins the race. Then suddenly, this college student who was reviled in the newspapers for not running on Sunday, is now headlined as Scotland's greatest sports star, even a national hero. People cheer madly at parades in his honor. Speaking invitations pour in. Newspapers scramble to report everything the young Scotsman does. Sometimes hundreds are turned away at church doors where he is scheduled to speak because there is no more room.

A few days after winning the gold, Eric gets his Bachelor of Science degree from Edinburgh University. He decides to stay one year longer to study theology at Edinburgh's Congregational College, but his weekends are booked solid with speaking tours.

A year later in July 1925 at age 23 he leaves for China to teach chemistry and become a sports coach to male students at the Anglo-Chinese college at Tientsin, China. These young men from well-to-do Chinese families, are possible future businessmen and leaders of their nation. Many receive Christ and ask to be baptized after attending Eric's Bible study classes held in his home after school hours. At age 27 he falls in love with Florence, a missionary's daughter, but must wait four years to marry her until she finishes nursing school in Canada. During one of his furloughs back to Scotland, Eric studies to earn his ordination as a pastor. But again Scotland so revers him, his weekends are packed with speaking engagements. People clamor to churches to hear him preach.

Back in China he faces tremendous challenges over the next years. Fighting seems ongoing in the countryside. Numerous scrimmages are now common among opposing Chinese factions – those of the Nationalists verses Communists – and the encroaching Japanese are attempting to overrun the villages.

Eric's mission board sends him to an area where many wounded are treated at the hospital and he is put to work as a nursing assistant. He also travels by bike to various villages to share the gospel. Eric is shot at, robbed, goes hungry, and makes dangerous trips hundreds of miles to negotiate for coal to heat the hospital. All this time he is separated from his family who live back near the missions station.

As Japanese violence continues spilling out over China, he believes it is no longer safe for his family to remain there. Since they have two young daughters and another on the way, he sends his family to Flo's parent's home in Canada while he stays as a missionary to help as best he can.

Saying their goodbyes before her ship sails, Eric whispers to Flo, "Those who love God never meet for the last time."

And the Japanese did come to his town of Tientsin declaring that no "enemies" would be allowed to leave China to return to their home country. He and others at his mission station had just two weeks to prepare for the move to the prison camp, choosing what meager belongings they could send ahead on trucks.

Along with 1,800 from 15 different nationalities, Eric was imprisoned in the Weihsien Internment Camp some 400 miles southeast of his city. While there he soon became known as Uncle Eric to the many children, including 97 parentless children of missionary parents from the China Inland Mission originally founded by Hudson Taylor. Many of the children suffered from malnutrition and dysentery and some died of typhoid as medicines were scarce. No one guessed that their internment would last for two years and one month – though Eric would not live to be released.

During their imprisonment many bonded into a community and worked together for the betterment of all in the camp. Each person used his or her expertise to help others. Eric was in demand both as a teacher and a member of the athletics department, working half a day at each activity. Teaching was the biggest challenge. They had no chalkboards and what paper they had was erased and written on over and over again.

Since Eric's college specialty had been chemistry and math, he used that knowledge to teach the children, many of whom hoped to enter university soon after their prison release. One such young girl's plight stands out.

When Eric learned she hoped someday to study chemistry at the university in London, he spent his evenings sketching the chemistry equipment she would need to do experiments; then he taught her how to conduct them. Even though she never touched real chemistry equipment, Eric's sketches were so accurate that she envisioned experiments, and when freed she scored so well on the university exam, she was accepted to study chemistry. Hers is but one story of Eric's servant's heart for those God put in his path.

Eric supervised athletic games, such as softball or running tournaments, and set up creative Friday Night Youth events. He was especially loved among young people.

Then Eric began to suffer from bad headaches, and like many others he was showing signs of malnourishment. Christmas 1944 came and went and afterwards he suffered a small stroke, but doctors did not have the equipment to diagnose further problems.

On February 21 he got out of bed to mail a letter to Flo, and their daughters Patricia, Heather, and Maureen. That night Eric

Liddell slipped into heaven, possibly resulting from a massive brain tumor. He was among the nearly thirty who died while imprisoned.

In time newspapers in Scotland and England reported the sad news: "The Flying Scotsman Dead At 43." "Scotland has lost a son who did her proud every hour of his life," the *Glasgow Evening News* reported. *Edinburgh Evening News* called him "One of the most admired men who ever took part in sports, whose devotion to his principles won him the highest esteem." Memorial services for Eric were held in numerous cities and villages throughout Scotland.

On August 7, 1945, almost six months after Eric is buried, the internees at Weihsien see an American B-24 bomber swoop down so low they can read the name on the side, "Armored Angel." Suddenly the plane climbs steeply, a door opens and seven paratroopers jump out. Rescued! Now they are going home. First, the sick, followed by the elderly, the children, and finally families. As they leave many make a last visit to a grave marked by a wooden cross – that of their friend Eric Liddell.

Only God knows how many lives he touched, how many came under his shadow, how many accepted Christ because of his servant's heart toward them. Notoriety? It meant nothing to Eric compared to his love for Jesus and dedication to loving others with the same type love as his Savior. He truly served others.[1]

Once while visiting Scotland, land of my ancestors, I saw some of the places where he was taught or preached, and I thanked God for the life of this hero of mine. Eric's shadow fell on me the first time I read his biography years ago. And it continues whenever I watch again the movie "Chariots of Fire."

Think about people who lived a life of serving whom you have never known personally yet their lives challenged and inspired you. Why don't you find the opportunity to share his or her story with someone, and be sure you emphasize why you admire what that person did or said. And the shadow will continue to lengthen.

Prayer: *Father, thank You for those who have gone before us and inspired us to do even greater things for You. Now help us to be good influencers and good stewards of the talents that You have given us. In Jesus' name we ask. Amen.*

Investing In Future Generations

I became a servant of this gospel by the gift of God's grace given me through the working of his power. Although I am less than the least of all the Lord's people, this grace was given me: to preach to the Gentiles the boundless riches of Christ, and to make plain to everyone the administration of this mystery [...] (Ephesians 3:7-9a).

"The soundest investment we can make for our future is to invest in each other."[2] – Mike Huckabee

Can a heroine you never met cast a shadow for good on you? Miss Henrietta Mears did to me. No, I never knew her but she did leave a legacy in me.

Her picture sits on my desk. A larger one hung on the wall behind the podium when I spoke at a women's conference at the Forest Home Christian Conference Center which she had founded decades earlier in California. I felt honored to even walk about her campground, where, by the way, a bear got into the garbage can at our cabin that night.

The parent publishing company she established to promote Christian literature, Gospel Light, published most of my books. How I wish I had known her. But she was way before my time.

In the fall of 1928 she accepted the position of Director of Christian Education at First Presbyterian Church of Hollywood and served there for thirty-five years, teaching and training thousands, including movie stars. Under her direction, the Sunday School grew to more than 6,500, the largest Presbyterian Sunday school of its kind in the world at that time. She spent twenty hours a week in lesson preparation for the thirty minutes of teaching she did for her young adult class which numbered around 600.

Her students called her "Teacher" and more than 400 of them went on to be influential leaders. For instance, Bill and Vonette Bright, founders of Campus Crusade for Christ, were greatly impacted by her life as they lived with her for ten years. Dr. Bright said, "She trained by her life, which is the most powerful way. You teach a little by what you say. You teach most by what you are."

A champion of women, she attempted to raise the consciousness of others to the value and giftings of women that should be used within and outside the church.

Miss Mears developed new Bible study techniques, trained leaders, published curriculum, conducted conferences, and prepared young people for the mission field. She wrote Sunday School literature targeted to her students' interests and abilities. She and three colleagues founded Gospel Light Press to print their lessons which were requested by churches of various denominations throughout the country.

She longed for a conference center where, in a beautiful outdoor setting, young adults could further their Christian growth. In 1938 she found it at a resort in the San Bernardino Mountains of Southern California where she and her board founded Forest Home Christian Conference Center. Over the years hundreds of commitments to Christ were recorded in the *Book of Remembrance* kept there. Revivals that broke out there in the 1940s had a lasting effect on several generations that followed.

Dr. Billy Graham, who said his evangelistic ministry was transformed in 1949 at a conference at Forrest Home, said of her: "She has had a remarkable influence, both directly and indirectly, on my life. In fact, I doubt if any other woman outside of my wife and mother has had such a marked influence. Her gracious spirit, her devotional life, her steadfastness for the simple gospel, and her knowledge of the Bible have been a continual inspiration and amazement to me. She is certainly one of the greatest Christians I have ever known!"[3]

Students who came under her influential teaching were involved in starting at least 50 other ministries. Campus Crusade, founded by Bill and Vonettte Bright, alone impacted thousands worldwide through mission outreaches, including *The Jesus Film*, reportedly seen by over 4.5 billion people by the year 2000.[4]

Young Life founder, Jim Rayburn, said, "She was my teacher long before she ever heard of me. When I began my work among young people I read everything she wrote and listened to everyone who could tell me about her. I tried my best to do things the way she would want them done."[5]

Dr. Richard C. Halverson, who served as chaplain of the United States Senate and was one of Miss Mears' "boys" at Hollywood Presbyterian said, "She was a giant of Christian education – not only in her generation, but in this century. I thought of her as a female Apostle Paul […]. There is simply no way to exaggerate her effectiveness as a teacher, communicator, and inspirer."[6]

More than 50 years after Miss Mears' death, Gospel Light Publishing was still producing Christian literature and books, even in other languages. Truly her influence, her legacy, her shadow impacted the world for Christ.[7] (Born 1890, she died 1963.)

Who was that special person who influenced you because he/she served others? A grandmother you never knew, but you heard plenty of inspiring stories about her life? A neighbor? A stranger? Someone you read about? Maybe it was a person you never knew yet his or her life's story caused you to become a better person or go for a different goal or change directions in your life? Let's thank God for those heroes and heroines.

Prayer: *Lord, thank You for the dedicated people who have come across my path, directly or indirectly – servants to You, inspiration to me. Thank You for those whose lives touched my heart and challenged me. Thank You for each of them – even those I have never even met – yet they pioneered paths that I can* *follow. Their shadow lengthened to inspire me, and I am grateful, O Lord Almighty. Amen.*

Each One Teach One

And whatever you do, whether in word or deed, do it all in the name of the Lord Jesus, giving thanks to God the Father through him (Colossians 3:17).

"Hunt out the deepest need you can find."[8] – Dr. Frank Laubach

Dr. Frank Laubach (1884-1970), a pioneer of the contemporary adult literacy movement, popularized the phrase "each one teach one," meaning the one taught to read teaches another to read. He spent 40 years as a literacy consultant to governments, church missions, and private organizations, working with native speaking teams in over 100 countries in more than 300 languages and dialects.

His epitaph aptly reads, "The man who taught the world to read." Through his Laubach Literacy method, several million people have experienced the joy of reading for the first time. The story behind the story of literacy goes like this:

Frank Laubach graduated from Princeton, earned a Master's and then a Doctorate from Columbia University, and went on to Union Theological Seminary. In 1915 he was commissioned by the Union Congregational church to serve in the Philippines as a missionary and to teach at the Union Theological Seminary in Manila. He also worked among Christian Filipinos, establishing churches and teaching them.

In the 1930s when working in the Southern part of the Philippines with the Maranao tribe, he realized literacy was a necessary tool for improving their lives. Since they were suspicious of him at first, he lived among them, listened to them, and learned their language. He noticed they seemed sad because when loved ones moved to another village there was no way to for them to keep in touch; they had no written language.

Dr. Laubach devised a written language for them by sorting out the 16 sounds of the Maranao language, using our Roman alphabet. He assigned one letter to each sound: twelve (12) consonant sounds and four (4) vowel sounds, and used pictures to help them remember each. People learned to read and write in two weeks or less. But when money became tight and teachers could no longer be paid, the old chieftain refused to accept that because there would be no teachers his people would never learn to read.

He declared, "If I can learn, anyone can learn. Let each one who learned to read, teach someone else or die." The "Each One Teach One" concept was born. "While Dr. Laubach spent his life in service to mankind, he was always encouraging others to "hunt out the deepest need you can find."[9]

What an awe-inspiring example of reciprocal living! Talk about serving and influencing! Challenging, isn't it? But each of us can serve someone, if we stay open to God's divine possibilities. He yearns to use us, too, in our own unique way and in our own sphere of influence.

Prayer: *Almighty God, You are so creative in the ways You teach us. Help us tap into Your great resources to become better stewards of what You have made available to us. Sharpen our minds and skills and equip us to carry out Your plan for us to help and serve others. Amen.*

Think On These Things

- When reading biographies of someone you have never known, who has inspired and challenged you the most? Why?
- Name the qualities you admire.
- Has your life or attitudes changed because of their example?
- Have you thought of someone you can serve?

Part Eight

LAYING DOWN YOUR LIFE FOR ONE ANOTHER

My command is this: Love each other as I [Jesus] have loved you. Greater love has no one than this: to lay down one's life for one's friends (John 15:12, 13).

"The words are everywhere. They have become America's favourite, bittersweet, and articulate bumper sticker [...] but they resonate further than that. For they are also the words that closed a remarkable conversation on 11 September between a man called Todd Beamer and Lisa Jefferson, a telephone switchboard operator. The words are: 'Let's Roll'"[1] – Ed Vulliamy

When four commercial airlines were hijacked in coordinated attacks by Islamic terrorists associated with al-Qaeda, using airplanes as their weapons, on September 11, 2001 almost 3,000 died in a field in Pennsylvania, in the Pentagon, and at the New York World Trade Centers, including first responders.

Here is the story of just one of those planes. Everyday folks. Going about their daily activities in their homes, workplaces, communities, travels – just doing what they always do. But sometimes they consciously make an ultimate sacrifice that tremendously affects and changes the lives of others.

When Todd Beamer boarded United Airlines Flight 93 at Newark Airport on September 11, 2001, he never dreamed that he would make a decision eighty minutes later that would cost him his life while saving the lives of perhaps hundreds.

As their flight was taken over by hijackers who claimed to have a bomb, he and fellow passengers found themselves victims of a national terrorist plot. Todd, along with several other courageous passengers, stormed the cockpit, bringing the plane down in a remote field in Pennsylvania – probably avoiding its final destination for crashing into the United States Capitol Building or the White House.

A few weeks later when his widow, Lisa Beamer, was interviewed she was asked, "Why did he do it?" She answered, "Todd was just an ordinary guy. He was extraordinary to me and to his family, but to the world he was ordinary. And like any ordinary guy getting on a plane that day in a business suit he was able to do extraordinary things."[2]

During the commotion before the crash, Todd Beamer, not wanting to worry his pregnant wife, had called the company that provides the telephone service on United Airlines flights. Lisa Jefferson, the GTC telephone switchboard operator in a suburb of Chicago took the call. They talked for 13 minutes, and at Todd's request recited together the Lord's Prayer and Psalm 23 – Bible verses they both knew well. Later, she was to relate to the world his now famous words, "Let's roll!" as he and a few other men attempted to save their plane from the terrorists. Instead, it took a dive into the soil in Somerset County, Pennsylvania.[3]

In the aftermath of the attacks, Todd's pregnant wife, Lisa, made more than 200 media appearances in six months. She even received a standing ovation when she was introduced to a joint session of Congress by President George W. Bush. Whenever she gave interviews or speeches she told of Todd's strong life-long belief in God and that she knew Todd was in heaven.

"He wanted his life to count; he wanted to live the Christian life. Not just talk about it. He felt he didn't need to be a professional preacher to serve God. He could serve God in business – and maybe even make more of an impact on the world than he could by speaking from a pulpit," she later wrote.[4]

She and Todd had together taught a teens' Sunday School class, where she says Todd wanted the high schoolers "to develop biblically based, solid character, so no matter what situation they faced themselves, they could make the right decision."[5]

He regularly met with a men's Bible study group where they held each other accountable. The day Lisa joined others who lost family members on the downed plane at the site in the Pennsylvania field, they were allowed to leave some personal mementos on a hay-bale altar. She left notes of love from her family and among other things a book, *A Life of Integrity* by Howard Hendricks, which Todd and his friends had been using in their Friday morning breakfast study group. (See Howard Hendrick's story in this book in "Part Three: Mentoring One Another.")

"It is true that Todd and the other heroes aboard Flight 93 gave their lives that others might be saved […]. Even in the midst of the hijacking, right down to the moment when Todd uttered his now-famous phrase, 'Let's Roll!' the true desire of his heart and that of Jeremy Glick, Tom Burnett, Mark Bingham, and all the others aboard Flight 93 was to somehow get home to their loved ones. They didn't want to die," Lisa writes. "One thing I've attempted to balance is the sadness I feel at losing Todd with the hope I have in knowing that this world is only preparation for an eternity of joy beyond compare in heaven […]. The pain is real, but so is hope."[6]

"Todd was willing to live out his faith all the way to the end. Todd built his life on a firm foundation so that when the storm came on September 11 he didn't have to check the blueprints to see if everything he had built his life on was going to stand. He knew," Lisa added.[7]

Todd Beamer's heroic shadow fell on his family, friends and yes even on Lisa Jefferson, the telephone operator who says Todd's call to her was a turning point in her life – his words she would play over and over in her mind. Countless others who were once teens in Todd's Sunday School are no doubt living out the "integrity characteristics" Todd tried to instill in them. Several people received Jesus as their Savior at his memorial service.

When their plane plunged down in a Pennsylvania field near Shanksville, some 40 people aboard Flight 93 voluntarily gave their lives to save others. Heroes emerged beside Todd Beamer: Tom Burnett, Mark Bingham, Jeremy Glick, and other passengers and airline personnel with names of Lou, Rich, Alan, Sandra, Linda, William, and many others who will be enshrined in the hearts of grateful fellow Americans.

In a November 8th address from Atlanta's World Congress Center, President George W. Bush referred to Todd Beamer and the others in his conclusion:

> Courage and optimism led the passengers on Flight 93 to rush their murderers to save lives on the ground [...]. We will always remember the words of that brave man expressing the spirit of a great country. We will never forget all we have lost and all we are fighting for. Ours is the cause of freedom [...]. We've defeated freedom's enemies before, and we will defeat them again. We will no doubt face new challenges, but we have our marching orders [...]. My fellow Americans, let's roll.[8]

A Flight 93 memorial in Somerset County, Pennsylvania will carry the marker: "A common field one day. A field of honor forever."

Prayer: *Heavenly Father, thank You for sending Your Son to die for us and to go prepare a place for us in heaven. Thank You, too, for those here on earth who gave their lives for others. So many did on September 11, 2001 during heroic rescue efforts at New York's World Trade Center, the Pentagon, and a*

Pennsylvania field. Too many to name, but You know them. Bless and comfort all families who lost loved ones that day. Thank You for hope You have given us because of Jesus our Savior. In His name I pray. Amen.

Unity Amidst Death and Victory

If we live, we live for the Lord; and if we die, we die for the Lord. So, whether we live or die, we belong to the Lord. For this very reason, Christ died and returned to life so that he might be the Lord of both the dead and the living (Romans 14:8-9).

"The only way evil can triumph is for good folks to sit down and do nothing." – Rev. Norvel Goff

Nine people died when a lone shooter opened fire during a Bible study at the historic Emanuel African Methodist Episcopal Church in Charleston, South Carolina on the evening of June 17, 2015.

The murderer was a stranger who lived two hours away – a stranger who had been welcomed to the group and stayed during some of the prayers before beginning his massacre. The young and highly revered pastor Rev. Clementa Pinckney, a state senator and father of two, was among those killed.

Outrage and anger could have fueled raging race riots right after the senseless deaths of innocent African American Christians. But not for this church congregation, this people, this city. Instead positive things happened.

- As a show of unity, thousands gathered on either side of Charleston's main bridge one evening and marched toward the middle. When those from the Mount Pleasant side and the Charleston side met, they began to sing "This Little Light of Mine." Black and white hugged and cried together.

- When the large church doors reopened, welcoming the crowds, they were so many that hundreds stood outdoors, some with arms uplifted singing praises to God, joining voices with those inside.

- As Emmanuel's congregation sang, church bells rang throughout the "Holy City" as another reminder of unity – Charleston was nicknamed that because of the numerous churches there.

- On the morning after the attack, a florist felt a nudge from God that a car she saw on the highway as she drove to work fit the description of the shooter's. On her tip he was arrested and finally indicted on 33 federal hate crimes as well as nine counts of murder by the state of South Carolina.[9]

- At the shooter's first court appearance, some grieving relatives of slain church members stood to speak words of forgiveness to the accused man for his heinous crime.[10]

Think of the impact on the gunman and those in the courtroom the day church members who had lost loved ones told the killer of their forgiveness! Surely, they spread an enormous shadow reflecting God's redemptive love. (I am purposely not naming the criminal to keep from giving him the publicity he sought.)

"The only way evil can triumph is for good folks to sit down and do nothing," said Rev. Norvel Goff, who was appointed to preside over the congregation as he delivered a message during the healing process.[11]

Prayer: *Father, strengthen and enable us to stand shoulder to shoulder with our grieving communities when calamities occur. We grieve because of the senseless killing of innocents. May their lives be honored and remembered. May their good legacy be passed down from generation to generation, that they did not die in vain. Thank You for Your comfort. Thank You for the promise of everlasting life to those who know You. Amen.*

Heroes On A Train

Hear my prayer, Lord; let my cry for help come to you (Psalm 102:1).

"For the sake of each of us he [Jesus] laid down his life – worth no less than the universe. He demands of us in return our lives for the sake of each other."[12] – Clement of Alexander

American heroes. Three young men vacationing in Europe and travelling on a high-speed train just an hour from their Paris destination. Childhood buddies from California, two in the military and one finishing his last year of college. Then the unexpected happened. Before their journey ended they would spring into action to help avert a possible massacre.

Alek Skarlatos, Spencer Stone, and Anthony Sadler were on an Amsterdam-to-Paris train on August 21, 2015, when 22-year-old Skarlatos, a National Guardsman who had just completed duty in

Afghanistan, heard breaking glass and saw a suspect with a gun – an AK-47.

"Get him!" he yelled to his two friends as a loud noise shattered the quiet. The three rushed toward the man with the arsenal of guns. Spencer Stone made the first contact with the suspect who attempted to shoot. The weapon jammed. They wrestled, finally ambushing him and tying him up with the help of a British passenger, Chris Norman. But not without injuries to themselves.

Skarlatos had seized the suspect's rifle and hit him with the muzzle. Sadler explained to a reporter, "The three of us beat up the guy. In the process Spencer gets slashed multiple times by the box cutter, and Alex takes the AK-47 away."

During the fray to disarm the shooter, Spencer Stone, who serves in the Air Force, sustained injuries to his head and neck and multiple cuts including one on his thumb that was almost severed. He spent one night in the hospital. "If anybody would have gotten shot it would have been Spencer for sure, and we're lucky that nobody was killed, especially Spencer," Skarlatos said. The gunman was a Moroccan national![13]

These three American young men received from the President of France the French Legion of Honor award, their country's highest recognition. This for foiling a potential massacre on that Paris bound train. Knights of the Legion of Honor, a parade down the streets of Sacramento, California, and a visit to the White House as guest of the U. S. president.[14]

Last minute change of plans put them on this train on this day. And their shadow of bravery spread; lives were spared.

Perhaps you have done a heroic deed yourself. Or knew someone who did. Thank God for the outcome. Think of other ways you can serve someone, maybe not as dramatically, but by your influence.

Prayer: *Lord, thank You for selfless individuals who put their lives on the line for others by responding out of a desire to do what is right rather than considering first what it might cost them! Amen.*

Missionaries Who Live and Die Serving Others

And He [Christ] died for all, that those who live should no longer live for themselves but for Him [Christ] who died for them and was raised again (2 Corinthians 5:15).

"The promise of Jesus means two things to us: 1. He will go through our trials alongside us. 2. We will go to heaven to be with him when we die." – Gracia Burnham

What about missionaries who should be on a "hero list" for laying down their lives for others? Missionary families around the world still live in remote villages, learn the language of the tribal people, and share about a loving God who does not require sacrificing animals to their dead ancestors. Or serving gods with rules and regulations forbidding them to eat nourishing foods growing nearby while their children sometimes die of starvation. Some of these missionaries are involved in needed work outside an evangelistic role.

Martin Burnham was one. Martin and his wife, Gracia, served among the poor on the Philippine islands of Luzon and Mindanao for 16 years. An outstanding pilot, he flew people, food, medicines, fuel for generators, and other cargo into some of the most primitive areas in that part of the world. Gracia was the radio operator and loving mom to their three children.

Gracia says Martin "had the incredible gift of piloting airplanes and could put a loaded Cessna down in a small jungle clearing and get the plane stopped in the next hundred feet... Plus, he loved people. That's what made him want to use his piloting skills to make a difference in the world."[15]

In May 2001 while celebrating their anniversary in Manila, they were kidnapped by members of the terrorist group Abu Sayyaf, who demanded one million dollars for their release. For over a year they were captives, and for seven months of that time, they were marched through the treacherous jungle by their armed kidnappers – sometimes in swamps waist deep. For over three months they had to sleep on the ground until finally they were given a hammock, but Martin was often chained to a tree even then.

As they walked in sweltering heat, they recited Scripture aloud, especially recalling Psalm 100 and repeating the verse, "Serve the Lord with gladness," which was Martin's motto and watchword.

Gracia says they always knew the Lord was with them. In the natural she struggled when she felt stinky and dirty with no place to get a bath and no privacy of a bathroom, no clean clothes and often not enough food. She writes about trying to get comfortable while trying to sleep on the jungle floor. But as she writes about her sense of the Lord's presence, one is encouraged. Her faith in Him is challenging to others.

On June 7, 2002, after a pursuit in which Philippine soldiers attempted a rescue, Martin was killed during the gun battle, as was a fellow captive, Filipino nurse Ediborah Yap. Gracia was shot in the leg but evacuated by the military. After medical treatment and debriefing at the U.S. Embassy in Manila she was flown to Kansas City to be reunited with her children. Her story, *In the Presence of My Enemies* and *To Fly Again,* written with Dean Merrill, is a stirring testimony of her love and faith in Christ.

They were not targeted because they were Christians, she says, but rather they happened to be in the wrong place at the wrong time when a band of kidnappers wanted bargaining chips. Around the world, however, Christians are being persecuted and martyred for their faith.

During their hostage ordeal, the Burnhams lived by the Scripture quoted to start this chapter. "Greater love hath no man than this, that a man lay down his life for his friends" (John 15:13 KJV).

Have you been influenced by a missionary who gave his life for the sake of the gospel? Do you have friends who serve in other countries who you pray for regularly? "Some go, while some stay and pray," a friend told me as she described the family she undergirds with prayer.

Prayer*: Thank You, Lord, for missionaries who hear the call to go to the nations to win others for You. Thank You for those who use their talents in* *various ways to enable others to accomplish their destiny too. Help me be faithful to pray for them. In Jesus' name. Amen.*

Think On These Things

- Who are some of your contemporary day heroes? Why?
- Can you find the opportunity to tell others about one or more of them?
- Have you ever done a heroic deed?
- Who is your favorite Bible character hero? Why?

Part Nine

CARING FOR ONE ANOTHER – FRIENDSHIPS

Two are better than one, because they have a good return for their labor: If either of them falls down, one can help the other up. But pity anyone who falls and has no one to help them up. Also, if two lie down together, they will keep warm. But how can one keep warm alone? Though one may be overpowered, two can defend themselves. A cord of three strands is not quickly broken (Ecclesiastes 4:9-12).

"When we have committed to keeping one another, we can trust that we are out for each other's good."[1] – Graham Cooke

Friends. Genuine friends are there for you when you need encouragement, sympathy, comfort, and support. You often shadow one another. Sometimes you may sacrifice for the good of the friend in need.

Faithful friendship. How well it is illustrated when four men wanted to get their paralyzed friend to Jesus for healing. Unable to get into the crowded room where He was, they persisted by cutting a hole in the roof and lowering him down. Jesus not only healed the paralyzed man, he commended his four friends for their faith. (See Mark 2:1-13.)

Jesus had many friends. Among His twelve disciples, three were even closer – Peter, James, and John. It was the disciple Andrew who brought his brother Peter to Jesus. Women followed Jesus, some even contributing funds to His ministry. He felt "at home" in Martha's home in Bethany which she shared with her sister Mary and brother Lazarus. Jesus taught and mentored His friends whenever they were together, but He also enjoyed their fellowship.

Supportive friendships hold each other accountable. Jesus urged us throughout His ministry, "Come with me and become involved." Sometimes schedules will need rearranging. Friendships cost time, respect, agape love, and plenty of prayer, but genuine friends are worth all the effort, even when at times it seems inconvenient.

Keeper friendships. How do they work? How can we best care for and bless each other? Sometimes you shadow your friend. Other times he or she may shadow you – depending on how you share your giftings with one another. Your friendship may be long term or seasonal.

Here's how a long term friendship began for me when I was a young mom. It started one Sunday after church.

"Would you like to bring your family and your dinner and come to my house today?" Lib, asked me as we chatted after church. I'd never met her before and we were just visitors.

"I don't have enough food for all of us, but we could share," she added. "You look like someone I'd really like to get to know. Besides our children would enjoy some new friends too."

I never imagined what I was getting into that Sunday we lugged our dinner to Lib's house and spread it outdoors on a picnic table. The next week her family came to our home, bringing their dinner. We did this every Sunday for over a year. We were shy young moms living in tiny box houses on shoestring budgets while our husbands worked crazy shifts at Florida's newly established Space Center and were often gone days at a time. Between us we had seven children near the same ages. Lib and I were born the same week and the same year. Sisters in the Lord.

As our friendship blossomed and our relationship with the Lord grew stronger, we decided we needed to pray for our children on a regular basis. So at exactly 8 a.m. we prayed together on the phone, for just five minutes, every weekday morning – for 17 years!

After my husband retired and we moved away, Lib and I kept in touch by frequent phone calls so we could pray specifically. She never mastered the computer and she didn't like letter writing. And she would not get in an airplane to come see me. So I made many trips back to see her.

Our friendship lasted several decades. Not long ago on a Mother's Day weekend, her husband and four sons buried her between a giant oak and a blooming gardenia tree. "She, who loved flowers and plants, would have approved," one son wrote me.

Lib was my introduction to a Keeper friend. Whenever and wherever I moved I looked for a friendship like Lib and I had so enjoyed.

In the ensuing years I have "collected" some wonderful female friends who have offered me nurturing emotional support, advice, counsel, encouragement, and prayer coverage. In turn, I have done the same for them. While we have seen each other through trials and heartaches, we have also had a lot of laughs. The Holy Spirit has become the glue that's kept us together. I am amazed and astonished when I think back how God brought each one into my life. He knew how I needed their unique giftedness!

A bronze plaque in my entry hall, a gift from a daughter, reads "The Lord Is My Keeper" from Psalm 121 as a reminder of God's keeping power. In the midst of our family's challenges, steadfast friends have covered us with prayer and encouragement. A dozen of them called us in the middle of one hurricane before our phones went dead. Their care and prayer was linked to God's keeping watch over us even though these Keepers live in nine different states. There is no distance in prayer.

Prayer: *Lord, thank You for the gift of friends, especially those I count on who love me in trying times as well as smooth-sailing ones. Help me remember to thank them for their faithfulness. Help me to be a very faithful friend to them, too. Amen.*

Keeping Begins With God

The Lord is your keeper; The Lord is your shade on your right hand [...] The Lord will guard your going out and your coming in from this time forth and forever (Psalm 121:5, 8 NASB).

"Keeping begins with our own relationship with God."
– Graham Cooke

"The Lord is our greatest keeper, and the basis of all covenant relationships," writes author Graham Cooke. "Once we understand that God is our keeper, we can begin to keep someone else. As He is, so we are. We must learn the dimensions of how God keeps us, and what He wants to be for us. God has places He wants to take us; He has a role in the Kingdom that only we can fill."[2]

When you look up "keep" or "keepers" – just some of the 371 references in the Bible – you will see that generally the Hebrew words for "keep" means: to guard; to observe; to watch as a watchman; to protect; to wait; to treasure up (in memory); to keep (within bounds), or to restrain; to observe or to celebrate; to keep (sabbath or covenant or commands); to perform or keep (a vow).[3]

Yes, we are called to keep one another as God has kept us. The Bible warns: "Let each of you look out not only for his own interests, but also for the interests of others" (Philippians 2:4 NKJV).

Among my Keepers are women who are gifted as counselors, writers, homemakers, and career gals. Some are moms or grandmoms. Some are younger, some are older, and some are my age.

But all are prayer warriors. We have a Mutual Admiration Society of sorts.

Several have been in a keeping relationship with me for many years. We got involved in each other's lives. We felt "at home" with each other. I have found it is healthier to have more than one good friend, to keep me from getting co-dependent. After all, each friend imparts something unique into our relationship. To keep my friendships vital I make phone calls and send cards, e-mails, and text messages. I also keep a record of my prayers for them – how I prayed and how God answered.

Recently one of my Keeper friends was in Africa in ministry, another was in India, and still another in South America. One friend's son is in jail; another underwent serious surgery; two of my prayer partners have teen granddaughters with eating disorders/addictions. No wonder we need to persistently pray for one another and their families. My current long distant prayer partners Sally and Kate assure me on our daily phone calls, "I've got you covered in prayer for that." As I also pray for them.

One of my most cherished Keeper friends, Mary Jo, who lives 700 miles away, called me every day for a number of years after I moved back to Florida. Just to connect and pray. We had met when she took classes I taught at a Colorado Bible Institute. Before long she was driving me to speaking engagements and while there she managed my book table and prayed while I spoke. She called herself my armor bearer. We enjoyed fellowship and endless cups of coffee on those road trips through the mountains where we often saw elk, deer, or buffalo. Whenever she shared rich nuggets she had discovered in her Bible study, I encouraged her, "Go girl, go." Now as an ordained minister, she has served as a busy Pastor of Prayer at a large city church for over a dozen years. She recently finished writing her second book. Proud of her? You bet I am. We keep in close touch and her picture remains on my prayer board as I bring her daily before the Lord.

"In friendship, there are seasons when we put our friends first because it is their time to shine. We want to serve that call. And there are times when it tips the other way, and our friends are called to serve us. When we have committed to keeping one another, we can trust that we are out for each other's good,"[4] writes Graham Cooke.

You soon realize not all Keeper friendships are at the same level of reciprocation. Some friends have less time than others to keep in touch. Some have full-time jobs. Others travel with their ministries. Some are community volunteers. Several are full-time caregivers to ailing husbands or parents. Others babysit their grandchildren while their moms work, and the list goes on.

We try to choose our inner circle carefully – not negative, cynical, naysayers. Most of us want positive-talking-thinking friends. However, a word of caution: a close friend may someday let you down, despite good intentions. Forgiveness goes a long way toward restoration.

"Within the immediate circle of your friends, look beyond the wrong," advises one pastor. "Every friend I have has disappointed me in one way or another. And I have done the same to him or her.

But because there has been a willingness to overlook that, we still have a friendship. Love helps us stay at the task."[5]

Yes, a friend may betray you. Jesus Himself suffered betrayal from one in His close circle. One betrayed Him, one denied Him, one doubted Him.

When betrayed early in my Christian walk, I went crying to my pastor. With understanding and sympathy, he comforted me, but then he wisely quoted Psalm 41:9: "Even my close friend, someone I trusted, one who shared my bread, has lifted up his heel against me." Then he added, "Remember, too, with the rose comes the thorns." Of course, he prayed with me, advising me to allow forgiveness to cover the wrong.

Some friends are just for a season, but their impact on our lives is lasting. Whenever we've moved, I have found it difficult to keep some long-distance friendships going. However, now in our advanced technology age, keeping in touch is much easier.

Yes, it will cost you to be a Keeper. You will walk through spiritual battles with one another, through "drama and trauma" and through tests, trials, and tribulations. But you will also have some victory days to celebrate.

Here is a Biblical admonition for those wanting to be Keepers: "[P]ut on a heart of compassion, kindness, humility, gentleness, and patience; bearing with one another, and forgiving each other [...] just as the Lord forgave you, so also should you. [...] [P]ut on love, which is the perfect bond of unity" (Colossians 3:12-14 NASB).

I have heard it said that a woman needs several kinds of friends, among them:

1. The trusted confidante – you can trust telling her anything; she keeps confidences.
2. The older friend – a mentor to you; has children older than you; gives wise advice.
3. The younger friend – one you can encourage; see yourself as you once were.
4. The mommy friend – has children near the same age as yours; can count on her to understand your nitty-gritty situations; rescues you in tight situations; does projects with you.
5. The career friend – when you work outside the home, having an "office pal" helps you to brainstorm or discuss ideas and problems.
6. The fun friend – your goofy, laid-back friend with whom you can laugh and enjoy life a little more fully. She doesn't judge you when your spontaneous ideas cause her to consider them and laugh with you.

We all need some joy times. Joy is mentioned over 200 times in the Bible. Can't you just picture Jesus experiencing great joy as He went about teaching, healing, enjoying fellowship with His disciples shadowing Him? In the Bethany home of Martha, Mary, and Lazarus, He seemed to have "en-joyed" the comradery of friends who lavished their hospitality on Him.

Today men are said to generally have less close ties with friends than women. One survey shows men tend to have: "convenience friends, who exchange helpful favors but don't interact much otherwise; mentor friends who connect through one man's tutelage of the other; and activity friends." The latter could involve sports or other shared activity interests. One author writes, "The theory holds that men tend to drift apart whenever the shared convenience, mentorship, or activity ends."[6]

However, in Christian circles, many men take advantage of opportunities to be in accountability groups or Bible studies where true friendships blossom. For example, since the early 1990s thousands of men have been involved in Promise Keepers gatherings which emphasized discipleship and evangelism, and closer friendships resulted. Today one of my former pastors conducts two "men only" groups each week in his home where accountability is a priority among them. Jesus, of course, set an example with twelve male friends whom He discipled.

Paul admonished the early church that "the members should have the same care for one another" (1 Corinthians 12:25 NASB). The same care! What can you do to show care to your friends? To encourage them? To help or benefit them? What caring thing can they, in turn, do to help you?

When I think about Lib, my first Keeper friend, I thank God for her boldness in asking me to lunch, even if I did have to bring my own. Because you see, we became forever Keeper friends. And we shadowed each other in different ways.

So, let's go help shadow those unique people in our lives – our treasures, our special friends.

Prayer: *God help me to strengthen my Keeper friendships so that others will see You through our unity. Bring the people of Your choice into my life at the right time and help our relationship to be what You desire it to be. Help me not to yield to immoral influences or destructive relationships. Please help me to follow Your biblical truths and principles. Please stir up the creativity in me so I can use my gifts and talents to the best advantage for Your Kingdom's purpose. I ask in Jesus' name. Amen.*

Think On These Things

What do you want in a Keeper friend? I interviewed men and women who told me what they desired in a friend and what they would do as a friend in return. It amounted to reciprocal friendships. Some said an ideal friend would be one:

- Who watches in prayer for me and allows the Holy Spirit to tell her how to pray.
- Who guards and keeps my confidences.
- Who believes in me even when I make mistakes.
- Who trusts me with her confidential information and prayer requests.
- Who gives me godly advice.
- Who helps me make wise decisions.
- Who lovingly corrects me.

- Who keeps in regular communication – via personal contact, phone, e-mail, or text.

- Who celebrates with me when I have a reason.

- Who helps me have fun on ordinary days.

- Who dreams dreams with me/for me (and I with her).

- Who covers an offense with love, understanding, and forgiveness.

Now let us carefully check out our motives before going into deeper friendships. Consider:

- Are we willing to have a mutual friendship?

- Are we willing to take the time to cultivate the friendship?

- Are we ready to allow someone to talk to us honestly about areas of our life that might need improvement?

- Can we truly be prepared to forgive?

- Can we not get jealous? Can we refrain from gossip?

A suggested prayer: *Father, thank You for the friends You have given me. Help me to be more sensitive to show them care and concern. Forgive me for times I have not been such a great friend. Or I was short with them. Or judged them wrongly. I honestly want to honor them and be there when needed. Give me compassionate and creative ways to stay connected that will be beneficial to us both. Amen.*

Part Ten

INFLUENCING FROM THINGS OTHER THAN PEOPLE

But Mary treasured up all these things and pondered them in her heart (Luke 2:19).

"With God, nobody is hopeless."[1] – Franklin Graham

Things often influence us. When pondering the word "things" we may think first of inanimate objects, those without life, like a possession. A thing can also refer to a thought, information, a deed. In more than a thousand places in the Bible "things" are mentioned: new things, hidden things, mighty things, wonderful things, good things, heavenly things, proclaimed things, pleasant things, valuable things, precious things, detestable things, wicked things, righteous things, things given, things spoken, other things, and many additional ones.

Illustrations in this chapter highlight people who, using their God-given talents, created "things" that left a shadow of influence over thousands of others through the years. Can a gigantic painting completed centuries ago cast such a shadow? Don't dismiss the idea until you think back over your own experiences.

Mine was viewing the Dutch artist Rembrandt's "Return of the Prodigal Son," finished in 1669, one of more than two million art works in the Hermitage Museum in Saint Petersburg, Russia. Twenty of us Christian women were following our tour guide as she chose what she considered the most important ones for us to see.

When we came to "The Prodigal," three of us were so awestruck by its powerful message that we asked the guide to let us stay and meditate on it while she took the group on to view other marvelous works. I stood glued to a spot to take it all in.

Studying the enormous painting – eight feet high by six feet wide – I tried to identify those depicted. The painting is the artist's interpretation of those in Jesus' parable about a sinful son, who after squandering his inheritance in a faraway land, decides to make his way home to beg his father to let him be just one of his servants. As Jesus tells the story, "So he got up and went to his father. But while he was still a long way off, his father saw him and was filled with compassion for him; he ran to his son, threw his arms around him and kissed him" (Luke 15:20).

Rembrandt uses mostly darkness in this rendition, but the primary light is on the face of the father whose hands rest on the back of his returned son. We don't see the son's face for it is buried in his father's bosom as he kneels at his feet. The contrast is there: the father in his rich scarlet robe, the balding son in a rag-tag drab garment and wearing only one worn shoe – having traveled a distance from feeding pigs. The servants stand nearby, and we see some color there. But lingering in the dark background is the eldest son, jealous of his returning brother's reception home.

In the biblical account, his father says to the servants,

"Quick! Bring the finest robe in the house and put it on him. Get a ring for his finger and sandals for his feet. And kill the calf we have been fattening. We must celebrate with a feast, for this son of mine was dead and has now returned to life. He was lost, but now he is found." So the party began (Luke 15:22-24 NLT).

The father's bright face readily expresses grace, mercy, forgiveness, acceptance, blessings, and much more that love encompasses. One tour guide swept her group past us, saying, "That Rembrandt is about a fable, and you don't need to see it."

This is not just a 300-year-plus painting but rather a reassuring message – a dramatic presentation of the forgiving and accepting love of God the Father. One who welcomes all repentant returning children. I silently thanked Him for His love of prodigals everywhere. For giving us His second-chances in life.

"What are You trying to say to me?" I asked Him after meditating on the painting for a while.

"I long to welcome home so many more of my prodigals. I love them. My Son died for them. Will you pray for them?" He whispered to my heart.

"Yes, Lord. I will."

I returned from Russia with a burden to encourage believers to keep praying their prodigals back to God's fold, back home. A few years later I co-authored a book *Praying Prodigals Home* with stories from parents I interviewed across our nation whose prayers for their prodigals had been answered. Some of the petitions they had prayed were also included.

Whenever I spoke for Christian groups I shared about the prodigal son from Luke 15, encouraging parents to keep open hearts and open arms even if the child did not yet ask forgiveness. The wait for them to come to their senses, as the prodigal son finally did, can be heart-breaking, difficult, and longer than a parent hopes. But keep praying, I urged, because it is not God's will that any perish. (See 2 Peter 3:9.)

One Sunday morning when I was speaking at a church in a northern state, I stopped abruptly during my message to say, "Some parent needs to hear this. Prodigals are going to start coming home, suddenly. Yours is one of them. I don't know who you are." A mother sitting near the front told me afterwards, "I believe that for my daughter. I take it. I take it." After the service I asked the pastor to let me know if there were results from that unexpected word about returning wayward ones.

A few weeks later I got a letter from the mother who had claimed her prodigal daughter. She included a copy of the letter her estranged daughter had written asking her mother's forgiveness and begging to come home. Guess when she wrote the letter? During that hour we were in church, when her mother believed that word was for her! After all, she had already invested months in praying. What a wonderful answer to a mother's prayer.

When I had absorbed the message of a 17th century artist, the most important shadow that fell on me was a new commission from God – to stand with brokenhearted parents believing for the return of their children and grandchildren.

And that shadow goes on and on because our book *Praying Prodigals Home* (co-written with Ruthanne Garlock) is published in other translations, even in Chinese.

Do you remember seeing a "thing" so spectacular or experiencing a "happening" so out of the ordinary that your heart was gladdened? And you were left with some wonderful memories to recall when you needed the inspiration they invoke.

Climb into your "thinking chair" and ask God to help you recall a time when a shadow other than a person impacted your life. It's there, just bring it back up. Then go tell your special experience to other somebodies. Let it fall on them.

Prayer: *Thank You, Father, for this wonderful parable Jesus related about Your love for even wayward children. Now Lord, I thank You that You love my prodigal more than I do. Thank You for bringing the right people across her path to help bring her back to You. Lift the veil of deception off her eyes. Give me the hope I need, the patience I need, and the prayers I need until that grand day comes. Prepare me to receive her! Thank You that my precious Savior died for her and for me. Amen.*

A 300-Year-Old Book Still Influencing

For what is our hope, our joy, or the crown in which we will glory in the presence of our Lord Jesus when he comes? (1 Thessalonians 2:19a).

"The time of business does not differ with me from the time of prayer; and in the noise and clatter of my kitchen, while several persons are at the same time calling for different things, I possess God in as great tranquility as if I were upon my knees before the Blessed Sacrament."[2]

– Brother Lawrence, 17th century French monk

Envision a book that is 300 years old, has never been out of print, yet was published after the author died! It is titled *The Practice of the Presence of God* by a man named Nicholas Herman, known as Brother Lawrence, who, as a poor kitchen worker in a French monastery, discovered a secret about knowing God's presence.

Except for *Pilgrim's Progress*, there is probably not another piece of Christian literature that has had as much interest. An estimated 22 million copies of the original book have been printed in the English language alone. And it continues to be a Christian classic.

Born in France in 1614, this lowly peasant was wounded serving in the military. When he was 24 he joined a Carmelite Priory in Paris, taking the religious name "Lawrence of the Resurrection" and spent the rest of his life with this order. But because he lacked the necessary education to become a cleric, he spent much of his life at the monastery working in the kitchen or repairing sandals. He struggled to experience God's presence in a deep way even when facing confusion, noise, and opposition.

Finally, this humble man came to a point he felt the very presence of the Lord as much when working in a busy kitchen as in a church worship service. His deep peace and joy drew people from all walks of life who came to seek his spiritual advice and guidance. "How did he do it?" they asked.

The wisdom he gave them and that which he wrote in his private letters became the basis for the book *The Practice of the Presence of God*, which Father Joseph de Beaufort compiled after Brother Lawrence died in 1691. It was popular among both Catholics and Protestants, impacting such great men as John Wesley and A.W. Tozer.

His message: You can know God's presence wherever you are, whatever you do. Just practice until you achieve it. He wrote, "Think often on God, by day, by night, in your business and even in your diversions. He is always near you and with you; leave Him not alone." He cautioned against giving up: "We ought not to be weary of doing little things for the love of God, who regards not the greatness of the work, but the love with which it is performed."[3] The publishers have now revised and reissued this book under the title *Practicing His Presence*.

Why not ask God to empower us to seek the joy of His presence in the midst of our every moment and circumstance? It's a great goal to set; something to practice achieving, until like Brother Lawrence we can experience God's presence no matter where we are.

Prayer: *Lord, help me know Your peace and presence even when it seems a storm is blowing around me. Your Word says You never leave me or forsake me, but I need that keen sensitivity to Your presence like that 17th century monk came to know even in the busyness of his kitchen labor. Thank You for helping me reach that goal. In Jesus' name. Amen.*

A Most Popular Devotional

But encourage one another daily, as long as it is called "Today" (Hebrews 3:13a).

"The people who influence us most are not those who buttonhole us and talk to us, but those who live their lives like the stars in heaven and the lilies in the field, perfectly simply and unaffectedly. Those are the lives that mold."[4]
– Oswald Chambers

Kings, nobility, presidents, white-collar and blue-collar workers, homemakers, and college students – folks from many walks of life – have found the 365 devotionals in *My Utmost for His Highest* just the encouragement they need for each particular day. They read the same devotions for that day year after year after year.

Oswald Chamber's well-loved *My Utmost for His Highest* continues to be read by millions of Christians. It has not been out of print since 1927, when his stenographer wife, Gertrude, transcribed his teaching notes into the book ten years after he had died at the age of 43. More than 13 million copies have been sold worldwide.

One year when our pastor learned that our nation's president was reading it daily, he encouraged our congregation to also read *Utmost* and to pray for our president as we did. I felt my prayer life expanded as I did.

Chambers, born in Aberdeen, Scotland, a gifted artist and musician, planned to study art, but while at the University of Edinburg, he felt called to study for the ministry. He left for Glasgow's Dunoon College where he remained for nine years as a student and tutor. In 1906 he came to the United States, spending six months teaching at a Bible School in Cincinnati, Ohio. From there he went to Japan and on around the world.

During the last 10 years of his life, Chambers served as: traveling speaker and representative of the League of Prayer; principal and teacher of the Bible Training College in London; and YMCA chaplain to British Commonwealth soldiers in Egypt.

While serving as a chaplain during World War I to British soldiers on the front lines, he died from complications of an appendectomy in Cairo, Egypt on November 15, 1917.[5]

Dead at 43, but his shadow would continue to spread, even 90 years after his death because of a devoted wife's exemplary shorthand notes of his lectures. When the war ended, Biddy, as she was called, returned with their daughter to England in 1919 and began translating her massive notes into a book. Before his death she had helped him publish many pamphlets of his teachings, but this project for 365 devotionals was a massive undertaking. It took her three years to complete it. She wrote her sister, "I will never come to the end of my wealth of notes."

She produced 30 volumes of his teachings before her death in 1966 and never gave herself credit for any of them – only Oswald Chambers' name went on the cover.

The book's title comes from the first devotional reading, January 1:

My eager desire and hope being that I may never feel ashamed. We shall all feel very much ashamed if we do not yield to Jesus on the point He asked us to yield to Him. Paul says, "My determination is to be my utmost for His Highest."[6]

I wonder if you, too, have been encouraged or influenced by reading this classic devotional book. Perhaps one paragraph or just a sentence here and one there so grabbed your attention it caused you to be and do your utmost for Christ.

The written word has long been an effective tool to motivate believers to share the gospel message. Think about it. Martin Luther was moved by God to write the *Ninety-five Theses*. These and other writings by Martin Luther, John Calvin, John Knox, Jonathan Edwards, John Wesley, Charles Finney, and many who came after them, continue to inspire men and women to follow Jesus.

John Bunyan read Martin Luther's pamphlet on Galatians, and it brought about his conversion and inspired him to write *Pilgrim's Progress*, which has been translated into more than 135 languages. John Bunyan wrote it while confined in jail for 12 years for refusing to give up preaching. He died at age 59 in 1688, yet his book continues to be available in public libraries, even in a children's edition. Of course, these "things" – books or paintings – came through people using their unique creative gifts.

Prayer: *Lord, thank You for things created by other people which continue to inspire me today. May my talents be used in creative ways to bless others also. Thank You, Lord. Amen.*

Attempt Great Things For God

Therefore go and make disciples of all nations, baptizing them in the name of the Father and of the Son and of the Holy Spirit, and teaching them to obey everything I have commanded you. And surely I am with you always, to the very end of the age (Matthew 28:19-20).

Expect Great Things From God; Attempt Great Things For God – William Carey in 1792.

A book and a slogan, both things that figured in influencing the lives of thousands even now years later, because one man from England named William Carey caught a vision, cast a shadow. Often called the father of modern missions, Carey possibly had the most significant influence to the Protestant missionary movement of the 19th century than anyone. When Carey read excerpts of *The Last Voyage of Captain Cook*, his worldwide view expanded. To some who read the notable explorer Cook's book it was a tale of adventure, but to Carey it spotlighted the world's spiritual need.

By his early 20s, Carey had mastered Latin, Greek, Hebrew, and Italian, and was learning Dutch and French. While working as a shoemaker, he kept a book before him to read. One day, in the solitude of the cobbler's shop he decided, "It be the duty of those who are entrusted with the gospel to endeavor to make it known among all nations." And Carey sobbed out, "Here am I, send me!"[7]

Carey's career progressed from a shoemaker to a teacher to an ordained preacher within a few years. While attending a gathering of Baptist ministers at Northampton, Carey suggested that Christians should go to the nations to share the gospel. An older preacher told him, "Young man, sit down: when God pleases to covert the heathen, He will do it without your aid or mine."

But Carey persisted. This time it was his book that touched people. His book, by the lengthy title of *Enquiry Into the Obligations of the Christians to Use Means for the Conversion of the Heathen*, laid the foundation for future missions work for decades to follow. Not only did it include early church history but it listed information about the known world as to countries' size, population, and religions. He emphasized how he believed the world could be reached for Christ.

On May 30, 1792, he preached his classic sermon as he shouted the challenge: "Expect Great Things from God. Attempt Great Things for God." This challenging statement became a slogan among Christians even to this day.

Following this sermon, the Baptist Missionary Society was formed. The next year Carey, at the age of 33, left for India with his family to spread the gospel. Before he left he said, "I will go down, but remember that you must hold the rope." The funds of the Society were extremely slim so those in England would need to help support him with prayers and money – holding the rope, so to speak.

Little did he or they know that he would live in India 41 years, never to return to England. He spent much of his life learning various dialects, transcribing the Bible into those languages, then printing them on presses, and making them available to thousands.[8]

Once his printing office was totally destroyed by fire. Buildings, types, paper, proofs, and worst of all, the Sanskrit and other translations perished in the flames, none covered by insurance. Within a few months Carey got the printing presses rebuilt, and as he continued translating, the gospel was soon being published again in still another language.

When he died in 1834 at age 73, he had been responsible for Scriptures being translated and printed in 40 languages (the whole New Testament in 30 of those); he had been a college professor; had founded a college at Serampore; had established a botanic garden; had collected a museum of natural history which he gave to his college; had witnessed India opening its doors to missionaries; had seen an edict against *sati*, for which he had championed, finally passed, prohibiting the burning of widows on the funeral pyres of their dead husbands; and he had seen converts to Christ. Think about it – because he read a book that challenged him.[9]

Carey also buried two wives and several children there. It was not an easy life. But thousands are able to read the Bible in their own language because of his work and sacrifice. Christian historians still consider him as the one who helped launch the Protestant missionary movement.

Years ago my mentor shared one of Carey's famous quotes to challenge and motivate me. I have kept a framed copy of it beside my desk ever since: "Expect great things from God. Attempt great things for God."[10] (Some sources switch the sentences to read: "Attempt great things for God. Expect great things from God.")

Consider, ponder, reflect on *things* which have inspired and influenced you. Now go share what you gleaned from its take-away. Get excited by a sentence or two written even ages ago which penetrated your heart and soul.

Prayer: *Father, thank You that something written long ago can stir us to seek Jesus even more, and we in turn can let our lives touch others. Thank You for the Bible, the greatest written Word and for those people who have used it as their guideposts to inspire and give us hope. Amen.*

Think On These Things

- Look up some Bible verses that deal with the word "things" and see if you have some new take-away lessons.

- List a few favorite books which have influenced your life. Answer why and how they did.

- List special objects that have made your life happier because they represent something that profoundly touched you or left you a great memory. Example: a piece of jewelry, a sculpture, a doll, a souvenir from a favorite trip, a photo, an antique.

- Think of other things which have brightened your outlook on life. Example: a roaring ocean, a spectacular waterfall, a colorful flower garden, a busy street scene, a snowcapped mountain. Did it make you appreciate your Creator even more and inspire you to desire to share your experience? To impact or influence others?

Part Eleven

LEAVING A LEGACY IN OTHERS

But you are the ones chosen by God [...] God's instruments to do His work and speak out for Him, to tell others of the night-and-day difference He made for you – from nothing to something, from rejected to accepted (1 Peter 2: 9-10 MSG).

"Live the legacy you want to leave [...]. Legacy lives on in people, and people live on after you are gone."[1] – John Maxwell

When my friend Suzanne asked God recently what her new role was now that all her children were grown and gone from home, she felt He gave her a question back: "What can you do for Me that no one else can do?" After contemplating that for some time she had an answer. "Tell my story."

When she told me this, I thought of Bible accounts of people telling their stories. Remember the man Jesus cured by sending his demons into a herd of pigs – and they ran off the cliff and died? He had sometimes lived in tombs and whenever he had seizures, even chains could not restrain him. After Jesus delivered and healed him, He told him to go home and tell what had occurred. Scripture says, "So he went away, proclaiming throughout the whole city what great things Jesus had done for him" (Luke 8:39 NASB). The whole city heard his testimony.

Or take the awesome account of the Samaritan woman who went to draw water at Jacob's well at noon one day. She was living with a man who was not her husband, after having had five husbands. A Jewish rabbi sitting at the well asked her for a drink. It was Jesus. She carried on one of the longest conversation with Him recorded in the Gospels. He offered her living water, and she was the first one He told that He was the Messiah. Leaving her earthenware water jar, she hurried to tell the townspeople.

Scripture says, "Many Samaritans from that town believed in Him because of the woman's testimony, 'He told me everything I ever did'" (John 4:39). Not only did they accept her testimony, they invited Jesus to their village. After two days with Him, many more believed He was the Savior of the world, not just because of her testimony. Spiritual multiplication.

A testimony is "to tell something you know firsthand, or to authenticate a fact."[2] When we share our testimony we can testify to what Jesus has done for us and thus influence others.

You will find more than 500 references in the Bible where people are instructed to tell. For instance: tell the people, tell your son, tell your brother, tell the good news, and a lot of names of individuals who are instructed "to tell" also. Now let's tie that in to how we get a testimony.

"An inheritance is what you leave with people. A legacy is what you leave in them."[3] This profound statement by author Craig D. Lounsborough challenges us to think deeper. Our life's story can be the legacy we leave in others.

As followers of Christ, we have an even bigger story to tell. This truth became more real to me on my first trip to Israel during Christmas week in 1972.

Our group arrived at sunrise at a beautiful garden spot outside the main gates of Jerusalem. The open tomb before us was possibly the one where Jesus' body was laid after his crucifixion or at least like it. During a worship service to commemorate His resurrection, we sang a few songs, then a visiting pastor gave a short message.

"Remember how you were searched before you were allowed into Israel?" he asked. Did I remember! They had taken my camera and tape recorder for close examination and embarrassed me with a body search.

"But you smuggled something into Israel they could not take from you. It is not found in museums or any historical places. You smuggled Jesus into Jerusalem. Because Christ in you is the hope of glory," he said, quoting from Colossians 1:27.

Those of us on this Christian pilgrimage had brought the Spirit of the Living Christ into Israel with us.[4]

"Christ in you, the hope of glory." That's the legacy put in us for us to put into someone else. Our story will differ with each of our circumstances, the season of life we are in, and even in the choices and decisions we have made. But we should share it.

One year our pastor, Peter Lord, challenged us to practice telling our story. The idea was to zero in on how we had changed after we made Jesus the Lord of our life. He suggested we practice telling it in a reasonable time frame: ten minutes, five minutes, and just one minute.

Standing before a mirror and imagining we were speaking to just one person about our transformation, we could practice by talking about the most important change we'd undergone. He cautioned not to tell our whole life's story in one bang-up speech. Instead, we should try to stick to one theme – whether it was freedom from an obvious sin or a hidden one such as unforgiveness, or judging others, or occult involvement, or pride, or lying, or any number of issues that were displeasing to God.

"Just tell your story," he would say. "Tell what Christ did for you and the freedom you now enjoy. Make it so interesting others will want to know how Christ can impact them too."

When we allow the Lord to deal with personal issues hindering us, we indeed become overcomers. Paul wrote, "Yet in all these things we are more than conquerors through Him who loved us" (Romans 8:37 NKJV). The phrase "more than conquerors" means "over and above." It describes one who is super victorious, who wins more than the ordinary victory.[5]

Isn't that the story we want to impart to others? Right now, maybe you want to pause. Ask yourself what is my story to tell? How can I speak it with such clarity that I hit the bull's-eye, the intended target? What can I do in my generation to influence the future generation for the glory of God? Who can I influence for good?

My mom left us a great example to follow. She not only talked to her grandchildren about the Lord, she prayed for them a lot. In the mornings, she held up her two hands toward heaven and prayed aloud: "Lord, these ten fingers represent my ten grandchildren. Please help them to always love and serve You. Cause them to use their talents for the good of mankind. I plant prayers for their children, and their children to follow – those yet unborn." Then she would intercede for each personally as she called their names, bringing them before the throne of God.

Mom only lived to see her oldest grandchild married. Today as I prayed for her 16 great-grandchildren, scattered around this nation, with three living overseas, I thanked God for the prayers she planted for them as I added mine to hers. But I always thank Him for her role model. Someone has said that each of us as Christians has a destiny that carries the touch of God from past generations through our generation into the next generation.

The psalmist wrote, "One generation shall laud Your works to another and shall declare Your mighty acts" (Psalm 145:4 AMPC). "Even when I am old and gray, do not forsake me, my God, till I declare Your power to the next generation, Your mighty acts to all who are to come" (Psalm 71:18).

Prayer: *Thank You, Lord, for those who have planted prayers for us – even for our future. Please honor the God-inspired ones and help me pray ones that will even affect my descendants. Amen.*

Imparting to Your Family

All these are the twelve tribes of Israel, and this is what their father [Jacob] said to them when he blessed them, giving each the blessing appropriate to him (Genesis 49:28).

"I believe every person is born with an inner desire to achieve, create, and leave behind something beautiful [...]. God Himself, who is the greatest of all, instills within each man a little bit of Himself – that 'little flame' [...]. If it is activated by Jesus Christ, then God gets the glory for man's daring."[6] – Jamie Buckingham

Everyday folks. Going about their daily activities in their homes, workplaces, communities – just doing what they always do, often not consciously thinking about someone watching or getting encouraged by what they do or say.

A child picks up behavior patterns from mom or dad, or bigger brother, or even his peers. Sometimes parents provide the best of the best shadows for their children to follow. Mary, a mom of five, whose family I have observed for over 30 years, is an example of a dedicated mom who set out to help mold them for God's Kingdom, and in the meantime let her shadow spread. She wrote me a summary:

John and I were married six months after I graduated from college with my degree in nursing. I absolutely loved taking care of hospital patients. It seemed nursing and I were a good fit for each other.

About four years later, I gave birth to our first daughter, Esther. I gave up my nursing job and dedicated myself to taking care of her at home, but I made plans to return to work as soon as she was old enough. Then I got pregnant again, this time with twins, a boy and girl. What a challenge to take care of three children under 18 months in age! So, again I decided to delay returning to nursing until the children were older. However, our delightful Hannah arrived when the twins were two-and-a-half, so a nursing career began to take a rather permanent home on the back burner.

When Hannah was almost four years old, our little surprise child, Lydia, was born! Child number five brought much grace along with her, and our lives were very full. The children really kept me busy!

As always, my nursing career was patiently waiting for me, and I longed to contribute to the family income and try to save for their college educations. One day when they were at school, I was seeking the Lord in my basement prayer place.

God clearly spoke to me, "Give your nursing career to Me. I have plans to use your children all over the world and

I want you to stay home and pray for them. I will provide for their college education." So, I cried for a few days, but finally gave my nursing to Him. Later, He gave me a job as a School Crossing Guard, which I loved, so I could be at home when the children came from school.

Several faithful praying women helped me wage the battle for these children, helping us through one crisis after another and eventually launching them into their life's work.

Today, three of these children and their families are long-term missionaries, bringing practical aid and God's love to North Central Asia, Southeast Asia, and South Africa. One has served 19 years in a third-world country I can't mention. Another daughter living in a busy American city is a critical care nurse married to a cardiac device technician, and they serve the Lord faithfully. Still another serves the Lord in the marketplace on the West Coast.

Through all the struggles, God has been true to His word to me, providing for all five of them to graduate from colleges and showing Himself strong on our behalf in myriads of ways. God clearly told me He will take care of them wherever He sends them. So, I remind Him of that promise frequently and see His mercy and sometimes miraculous protection and provision displayed over our family.

I have marveled at Mary's resiliency – especially after her car was hit by a drunk driver while coming home from church one night. She spent painful months in a rehabilitation facility recovering, even learning to walk again. Or going 10 years without seeing one child who was serving the Lord thousands of miles away. I watched her walk with faith as each child needed funds for college. I greatly admire her, knowing that she and her husband open their home as the "hospitality house" to pastors, missionaries, and others who visit their church.

"Make yourself part of my shadow," a mother says to her young son in Jane Kilpatrick's *Every Fixed Star*.[7]

Parents are often the first and lasting influencers in families – whether for good or bad. Over 40 years ago, Yale conducted a study on how one person's life affects the lives of his children, and it focused on two men who lived in 18th century America. The godly one's descendants made great contributions to society, while the other's cost the government thousands. I choose not to tell about the man who was an atheist, and many of his children had some evil influences.

But here are the results of the godly one:

Jonathan Edwards (1703–1758) was a Puritan theologian. He was a leading figure in the First Great Awakening (1740-1742), which was the most intense outpouring of God's Spirit in American history at that time. Taverns closed, churches were crowded, and it was reported that 10 percent of New England came to Jesus Christ. He had a godly wife, Sarah. He fathered 13 children and did his best to influence them in the Christian faith. (Some records say he had only 11 children.)

Edwards had 929 descendants, and of those 430 were ministers, 86 became university professors, 13 became university presidents, 75 authored books, seven were elected to the U.S. Congress, and three were governors. One descendant was vice president of this nation. What a legacy.[8]

Prayer: *Father God, how we thank You for those people who had a positive and lasting influence on us – who loved us with unconditional love and who spurred us on to greater heights. Bless them. Give me the opportunity to someday thank them, whether here on earth or someday in heaven. Amen.*

Enlarge My Territory

The Lord is not slow about His promise, as some count slowness, but is patient toward you, not wishing for any to perish but for all to come to repentance (2 Peter 3:9 NASB).

"Daily I pray, 'Lord, please order every detail, every contact, every conversation, every point of communication, according to Your divine order for me today. Amen.'"
– Barbara James

Jabez. You have probably heard of Jabez among the men listed in the Old Testament family tree of the Hebrew tribes. His mother named him Jabez (pain), as she bore him in pain. He was "honorable" even above his brothers. We read about him in just two verses in First Chronicles. But his prayer legacy became more widely known when

Bruce Wilkinson wrote *The Prayer of Jabez* book which became a New York Times best seller. Jabez prayed like this:

> And Jabez called on the God of Israel saying, "O, that You would bless me indeed, and enlarge my territory, that Your hand would be with me, and that You would keep me from evil, that I may not cause pain!" So God granted him what he requested (1 Chronicles 4:10 NKJV).

Jabez was asking for a larger territory. For his border to be expanded. He wanted to do something great for God. I wonder how many of us actually pray like that. He wanted God to keep him from evil and from causing pain. He greatly wanted God to bless him – indeed. In the biblical sense, "to bless" means to ask for or to impart supernatural favor. When we ask for God's blessing, we are crying out for His unlimited goodness that only He knows how to give us. And we can pray this blessing for favor for others.

I had finished reading Bruce Wilkinson's book on Jabez, when shortly after the September 11, 2001 terrorist attack on our nation, I was on a crowded airplane. Before takeoff the pilot advised us over the loud speaker to get acquainted with our seatmates, to share family pictures, to really get to know some facts about them. Because, he said, in these uncertain days we might need to know that information. Was he preparing us in the event another airplane was hijacked and we would need to know our neighbor?

As we were preparing for takeoff, the 50-something-year-old man seated next to me closed his cell phone, smiled, and said to me, "Well, I just made a few million dollars with that call."

I laughingly replied, "What are you doing sitting so far back in the plane beside me? Shouldn't you be in first class?"

"Overbooked," he assured me. Six of his company men were on the plane too, he said.

Could this be a God-ordained opportunity for me? Well, I had a captive audience, and he had a listening ear. After he explained he had a burn-resistant invention he was going to Texas to test, I complimented him on his sharp mind and great skills.

"But we have a Creator God who gives us brilliant, witty ideas," I said. "I believe God inspired your thoughts and extended your territory. Sounds like your invention will benefit mankind, even globally," I told him. This grabbed his attention and he asked more questions. I tried to introduce him to our big God.

Between a few curse words, he told me bluntly he was not a believer but said his wife was very religious. Yet he was still shaken from the deaths of more than 20 from his New Jersey community who had perished in the Twin Towers collapse. He choked up when he told me stories about some of those he knew.

I asked the proverbial question, "If you had died that day, too, where would you be today?" While that jolted him, it gave me the opportunity to share about Jesus and how he, too, could have eternal life through Him. He just smiled and was silent a while.

Then, reaching into his wallet, he handed me a half-dozen pictures of his adorable 5-year-old daughter, as he bragged about the designer clothes he had bought her. Sighing, he admitted he was so busy travelling, he hardly got home to see her. I strongly challenged him to find the time for her and his beautiful young wife, because someday he would not want to live with regrets. We had a delightful conversation all the way to our destination – and we enjoyed each other's company, though we would never meet again.

After landing as we walked toward baggage claim, I pointed to the airport bookstore ahead. "Go in there and get *The Prayer of Jabez* book and then start reading your wife's Bible when you get home," I said with a wave. He nodded, smiled, and waved back. I won't ever know the results of our conversation, but I believe God had an encounter planned for both of us that day!

Would you like to consider saying the Jabez prayer yourself? Ask Him for more territory? More influence for Him? Ask, too, for His blessings. For a legacy to leave in someone. And yes, even expect God's blessings for today.

Sometimes we influence without realizing it, even to strangers. My friend JoAnne and I were attending a Christian conference in a large city when we decided to stop for afternoon tea at an old-fashioned drug store. As we sat at the soda fountain counter, she began to tell me a miracle story she heard on a Christian television program earlier that week. She gave every detail she could remember about the woman's healing from an incurable disease. I asked questions now and then for clarity.

I noticed a man sitting two seats away from us with a newspaper in front of his face. As soon as JoAnne finished telling me again how much Jesus loves us all, not just that woman on television, the man threw his newspaper down on the counter.

He shouted, "All right, already. I will get baptized. I will, I will. Sunday." He literally ran out of the drug store. JoAnne and I looked at each other in amazement. We offered a short prayer for that man, who obviously was on his way back to the Lord. Who knew what a conversation over a cup of tea could bring. God had unexpectedly expanded our territory.

Another time, JoAnne and I were on an airplane headed for Europe where I had speaking engagements. The man sitting next to me told me that his dad was occupying the aisle seat across from him and that he and his mother were trying to get him back to their home in the Middle East because he had undergone lung surgery in Houston. But into the night the ailing dad required more attention from his son and airline attendants. An hour and a half before we were to land in Frankfurt where they needed to change planes, he quietly died. Some passengers sitting nearby went into what I called "the crazy panic mode," chattering loudly, some demanding to be moved. One airline attendant was crying, even while trying to calm or reseat passengers.

JoAnne and I prayed quietly for peace and calm to come out of the confusion. Then she began to sing softly in her prayer language, then to hum some well-known hymns. Quickly the atmosphere changed. Peace seemed to permeate the cabin. People stopped demanding attention from airline attendants. I tried to comfort the son as his eyes focused on his dad's body, now covered in a sheet. His mom continued to sit next to her deceased husband, quietly grieving.

In Frankfurt that evening, JoAnne and I reflected on our experience. She said, "I guess God chose us to be the ones to sit in that strategic spot, knowing we would offer condolences in their heartache and be praying for them."

Sometimes we hesitate to step out of our comfort zone because we fear making mistakes. We don't want to feel insecure, vulnerable, displaced. True, when facing a new experience, we might not know how to react exactly right. But we can ask for God's direction and keep trying.

Prayer: *Lord, order my steps. Give me the right words to say when I need it. Help me not to be afraid to speak to strangers about a loving Heavenly Father who gave His Son for our salvation. Thank You, Lord, for situations in our life when You come through when we need Your guidance and wisdom. Help us to be open when You expand our borders. Amen.*

Influencers for Good

Now we ask you, brothers and sisters, to acknowledge those who work hard among you, who care for you in the Lord and who admonish you. Hold them in the highest regard in love because of their work. Live in peace with each other (1 Thessalonians 5:12-13).

"What could be greater than to be chosen by God to touch someone's life who will go where you cannot go and do what you cannot do?"[9] – Terry Crist

An influencer for good. Not just someone we can imitate from a close-up position. Not even one we can follow around and be mentored by him or her. These "influencers" may have no hands-on involvement in our life. Yet their influence affects the choices we make.

When I read who greatly influenced Billy Graham's commitment to Christ, I was struck with the domino effect – the "Shadow Falling on One to Another" concept – eventually affecting millions. I have no way of knowing if all the "influencers" happened exactly like this but it is fascinating to realize how it can work. It started when a teenage boy named Dwight Moody was converted in a shoe store on April 12, 1855 and was later hailed as the greatest evangelist of his century. Here is how it goes:

A layman by the name of Edward Kimball led Dwight L. Moody to Christ. Dwight went on to be one of the greatest preachers of modern [19th century] history. It was D.L. Moody who impacted F.B. Meyer, and Meyer touched Wilbur Chapman. Chapman partnered with Billy Sunday, and Billy Sunday had a major impact on Mordecai Ham. Mordecai Ham felt like a failure in his ministry and decided to quit. He felt burdened to do one more revival circuit. A 16-year-old boy with little interest in the revival was persuaded to go to one of the last services. That boy was named Billy Graham.

How many people would know who Mordecai Ham is? For that matter, how many people have ever heard of Edward Kimball? Edward Kimball is as much an heir to the fruit God produced as D.L. Moody and Billy Graham are. God is not interested in what you can do. God is interested in your obedience and faithfulness.[10]

When we read about renowned people, we can easily become intimidated into thinking our talents or abilities are not valuable. Friend, we do not have to have some grand, famous role. Nor should we compare our giftings. Have you ever considered that you – yes, you – can be a history-shaper when you influence the lives of others for good?

Let's rejoice over our own unique niche in life and look for ways to share our capabilities with others. Now, if you are ready, ask Him to send those for you to influence for Him. God can use whoever, wherever, whenever. Are we ready to volunteer? What legacy will we impart?

This quiz might jog a memory as it did mine when I read it in a newspaper some years ago. It went like this:

Can you list the five wealthiest people in the world? The last five winners of Miss America contest? Five winners of the Nobel or Pulitzer Prize? The last five Academy Award winners for the best actor or actress? The last five World Series winners?

The answer was: few of us remember the headliners of yesterday, even though the people were the best in their field. Applause dies. Achievements are often forgotten. But here is an easier quiz. So, try this:

List a few teachers who aided your journey through school. Name three friends who helped you through a difficult time. Name five people who taught you something worthwhile or valuable. Think of a few people who made you feel appreciated and special. Think of five people you enjoy spending time with. Name a half dozen heroes whose stories have inspired you.

"The people in your life are not the ones with the most credentials, most money, or most awards. They are the ones who cared."[11]

Let's thank God for the ones who cared. Then during some "reflecting time," we may even write a letter, make a phone call, or write out a one-paragraph summary of what each of those people meant in our life and record it in our journal. How about we also try to find a way to pass it on?

Prayer: *Thank You for those who imparted to me and gave unselfishly of their time and caring. Show me ways to acknowledge their faithfulness to me. I thank You they did not give up on me. Bless them. In Jesus' name. Amen.*

Think On These Things

- Considering the thought that "a legacy is what you leave in someone," to whom would you like to leave a legacy? Spend some thinking and prayer time, then write out what legacy you would like to leave them. Be specific.

- What are some goals to help you do that?

- Find someone to whom you can impart: your wisdom, your time, your energy, and even your resources, and pray she/he will then out-distance you in their field of influence.

- What prayers can you voice on behalf of others?

- Ask the Lord which opportunities He wants you to embrace to bring the truth of the gospel to people you will meet.

- Ask Him for strategies to reach these people.

- Pray for safety and protection over future generations.

- Practice Christ's teachings. To practice is to do something again and again, with a goal of proficiency. The Scripture reminds us: "And this is how we may discern [daily, by experience] that we are coming to know Him [to perceive, recognize, understand, and become better acquainted with Him]: if we keep (bear in mind, observe, practice) His teachings (precepts, commandments)" (1 John 2:3 AMPC).

- All of us have a story to tell. Think about sharing yours – whether it is about you, a close relative, or a public figure whose life inspired others. While we live in an interconnected world, heartwarming personal stories help give us encouragement and hope.

Part Twelve

REMEMBERING THE PAST

The Lord will rise up [...] To do His task, His unusual task, And to work His work, His extraordinary work (Isaiah 28:21 NASB).

The LORD will fulfill his purpose for me (Psalm 138:8a ESV).

"Memories are the key, not to the past, but to the future."
– Corrie ten Boom

Looking back over your life, I am sure you have some precious memories of people, experiences, and places which greatly impacted you. Perhaps reading or hearing stories about your forefathers' adventures stirs a new appreciation for where you are now.

The Israelites were asked to remember their history. Their past was celebrated and recounted to successive generations. Memories connect our past with our present, joining yesterday with today and the future.

Perhaps other people did things that influenced you, though you never met them. When recalling a few happy memories, I am once again mindful of God's faithfulness in helping me fulfill my destiny. How about you? As I travel down memory lane a bit, I hope it triggers a great remembrance for you, even a nudge to write down your own special memories too.

What an awesome adventure I have had – travelling to 26 nations, speaking to audiences in 12 countries and 47 states, as well as on more than 350 radio and television stations. Ever since I could hold a pen in my hand I wanted to write. I have now written or co-authored 30 books, exceeding a million copies in circulation, not counting those published in other languages.

At our Tallahassee high school graduation party, the church's youth pastor asked us to share our dreams for our future. What were our goals? Our hopes? My answer was simple. "To be a wife, mother, and a writer." And the Lord graciously granted that request.

I am an ordinary woman, raised by a single mom of four children, who ran a boarding house. I earned my journalism degree from Florida State University by working two jobs. After graduation, I married a Texan with a math degree I had met at FSU. With his Air Force duties behind him, he wanted to pursue an engineering degree from University of Houston. We both worked jobs for that goal: I, as public relations director for a downtown hospital, while he worked for a centrifugal pump company. He studied long hours, and I typed up his homework, struggling to read his handwriting about technical stuff that was almost beyond my comprehension.

Two years later we made our way to Central Florida where he was to spend almost 20 years as an aero-space engineer for NASA. We arrived there even before it was named Kennedy Space Center. (He did take a short job stint back in Texas.) After our three children were school age, I went to work as a feature writer and columnist for a newspaper close to the Florida Space Center. And so, my life of combining marriage, motherhood, and a writing career was fulfilled. Now for some memories about some of my exciting adventures.

An Astronaut Visit 45 Years Later

On January 23, 2015, I had the great opportunity to speak with former Apollo 13 astronaut Fred Haise and give him a copy of a 45-year-old newspaper clipping of an article I had written of my interview with him. In the accompanying photo, Haise and I are talking – I with my press camera strapped around my neck.

My husband, a NASA engineer, was on duty there on April 11, 1970, the day Fred Haise, Jack Swigert, and James A. Lovell, the mission commander, were launched into space headed for a moon landing. I observed the liftoff from outdoor bleachers reserved for the press while covering the event for the *Titusville Star Advocate* newspaper.

However, Apollo 13 never completed its intended moon mission. An oxygen tank on board exploded, leaving the crew without electricity and water – 200,000 miles from Earth. When smoke filled the cabin following the explosion, the astronauts were in extreme danger. Could they get lost in space?

President Richard Nixon had asked the nation to pray for their safe return. Our family was among those who attended some of the prayer meetings held in Brevard County, Florida on those suspenseful days. During the four-day crisis, the astronauts kept their heads clear despite severe cold and dehydration. At the Space Center in Houston, engineers, astronauts, and NASA personnel worked around the clock using their skills and expertise to save them. And they did.

In fact, some weeks later those astronauts came back to Kennedy Space Center to thank the personnel involved in their launch. Sitting in the newspaper office that summer day, I had a sudden hunch that they would probably be leaving from our local airport soon. Turning to one of the reporters sitting beside me, I said, "Grab a camera and let's go find an astronaut." I told my editor where we were headed. He waved us off with his "okay."

Sure enough, when we drove up, I spotted all three waiting to board their plane, but I chose to speak with Fred Haise while they waited. I flashed my Press badge and began to talk with him, taking notes, while Nancy snapped our picture. My article was published soon afterwards in one of the larger newspaper affiliates.

Forty-five years later my opportunity to speak with Haise again came backstage after he was the keynote speaker at a Chautauqua Assembly event in DeFuniak Springs, Florida – a town where my parents lived before my birth and where I was married. In fact, one of my daughters had taught in the very high school where he spoke to the Chautauqua audience.

As he lectured, Haise showed a video of a portion of their journey along with pictures of Kennedy Space Center. I recognized a few engineer friends in the control room photos. He explained how the astronauts had to use the lunar module as a lifeboat of sorts for the duration of the mission, though it was designed to sustain just two astronauts on the surface of the moon for a day and a half. They powered down to the lowest levels possible in order to conserve power. During their four-day ordeal, the astronauts endured with severely restricted water and food rations. And with limited power, the temperature in the lunar module was extremely cold. However, the Apollo 13 crew safely splashed down in the Pacific Ocean near Samoa on April 17, 1970, thanks to their skills, the efforts of the Houston space team, and God answering prayers. (See the movie Ron Howard did of Apollo 13.)

As I heard Haise speak that morning, my mind flashed back to that summer day 45 years earlier when I felt prompted to go after that special interview. During our conversation now I told him about the many people in our area who attended prayer watches held for him and his space travelers during their uncertain future. He listened closely.

A great remembrance for me and a great short "reunion" brought back lots of happy-time memories of the many space launches I covered in my writing years with the *Titusville* newspaper.

Commander Jim Lovell later commented about that journey. "As for me, the seven extraordinary days of Apollo 13 were my last in space. I watched other men walk on the moon and return safely, all from the confines of Mission Control and our house in Houston. I sometimes catch myself looking up at the moon, remembering the changes of fortunes in our long voyage, thinking of the thousands of people who worked to bring the three of us home. I look up at the moon and wonder, when will we be going back, and who will that be?"[1]

Prayer: *Lord, thank You for special encounters and for happy memories – all made possible because You, Creator of heaven and earth, orchestrate our events. Thank You for experiences that leave a shadow on us even years later. I was blessed. I am blessed. Amen.*

Beauty in Their Heart and Home

The LORD bless you and keep you; the LORD make His face shine on you and be gracious to you; the LORD turn His face toward you and give you peace (Numbers 6:24-26).

"I expect to pass through life but once. If therefore, there be any kindness I can show, or any good thing I can do to any fellow being, let me do it now, and not defer or neglect it, as I shall not pass this way again."[2] – William Penn

While on an outreach mission with 15 other American women in an Indian village high in the Guatemalan mountains, we distributed food, clothes, school supplies, and gospel publications to those who met with us in the rustic church. The nurses among us opened a temporary clinic, and the teachers, a small school. One morning our team leader, JoNell, and I rode in a flatbed truck with our interpreter as far as the dirt path led. Then we hiked the rest of the way up the mountain through fields of coffee trees, feeling we could almost touch the clouds as they rolled in just above us. Our goal was to reach a certain pastor's home.

He had asked us to come pray a blessing on his home and family. So, we happily entered his modest one-room hut with its simple tin roof and dirt floor where baby chicks scratched at our feet. The entire family lived in one room – without an indoor bathroom. I soon noticed a small coffee can holding a bouquet of white calla lilies – wildflowers which the pastor's wife had picked to bring beauty into her modest home. As we prayed together and sang praises, we felt the closeness of the Lord. Their home, lighted only by a kerosene lantern, was made more beautiful with wildflowers and their children's crayon drawings. Singing a hymn for us in their beautiful voices, they reflected their "Source" – Christ the Light of the world. And they cast their shadow on me which is still there years later.[3]

Maybe you, too, can remember a scene that touched you greatly. Why not write it down so that many more details come to mind?

Prayer: *Lord, thank You that You can make us happy regardless of our living conditions or circumstances, especially when we concentrate on what You have done for us in sending Jesus as our Savior. Thank You for these warm and precious memories when You help us to recall happy times. Amen.*

Discovering Special Scottish Landmarks

I will make Your name to be remembered in all generations; Therefore, the people shall praise You forever and ever (Psalm 45:17 NKJV).

The memory of the righteous is a blessing (Proverbs 10:7a ESV).

Where with intention I have err'd,

No other plea I have,

But, Thou art good; and Goodness still

Delighteth to forgive.[4]

– Robert Burns (written 1781)

Explore Edinburgh on our own? Our tour guide encouraged us to walk wherever we wanted to go in that ancient city one cool May afternoon. My sister Ann and I were in Scotland in memory of our late mother who never achieved her lifelong dream to come and check out her Lamont clan.

Without guidebooks, we walked the streets near our hotel, turning slightly off Royal Mile, until we came upon a building originally built in 1622. Carving above the door read: "Feare The Lord and Depart From Evil" while the other read, "Writers' Museum." Both signs intrigued me. We walked in and for 30 minutes we had the museum to ourselves.[5]

The building was dedicated to three of Scotland's most famous writers – Robert Burns (1759-1796), Sir Walter Scott (1771-1832), and Robert Lewis Stevenson (1850-1894). As a writer, I was delighted at this discovery. Our mother, who won awards for reciting long poems in her high school "elocution" contests, had encouraged us as children to read and memorize some of their works.

The small museum was crammed with pictures, etchings, busts, and memorabilia of the three writers, including Bibles, pipes, and walking canes. Rare books, Burns' writing desk, first edition books, and handwritten manuscripts grabbed my attention. I could hardly contain myself.

I touched what was permitted, sat where seats were provided, and recalled as many verses from these well-known writers as I could. I tried to imagine Robert Lewis Stevenson, ranked among the 26 most translated authors in the world, writing his famous children's poems.[6] Just that morning our tour bus had stopped in front of the house where he once lived and a little towheaded youngster came to the front window and waved at us.

When my children were young, I read to them from Robert Stevenson's *A Child's Garden of Verses*, and later they themselves read his *Treasure Island*. Robert Burns, known for his romance writing and poems, even composed the song "Auld Lang Syne." Sir Walter Scott, on the other hand, wrote novels, mysteries, and poems, and was appreciated by his countrymen for keeping Scottish history alive, even in his fiction.

During various seasons in my life, writings by each of them cast a wonderful shadow on me. My dad requested one of Robert Burns' poems be read at his funeral. (A portion is quoted above.) Now while looking over their treasured memorabilia in the museum I had a better feel for what their writing habits and challenges had been like. I also gained a new appreciation for my laptop computer and printer which I use when writing manuscripts.

Sometimes, however, when I read biographies of some individuals I have admired for their contribution to society, I may not always agree with their philosophies or lifestyles. But where would any of us be today except for God's grace and favor?

After we left the Writers' Museum, Ann and I headed back toward our hotel. We paused suddenly when we were standing in front of a picturesque townhouse built prior to 1490. The sign indicated it was where Rev. John Knox, the Scottish Reformer, once lived. When we entered, the museum guide told us we were fortunate because the home had only reopened to visitors that very day. What a happy surprise!

Knox lived from 1513 to 1572 and was known for spearheading the Protestant Reformation of Scotland and influencing the early Presbyterians from his pulpit in St. Giles Cathedral which was nearby.

He had been converted to Christ after he met two Bible-believing Christians, one by the name of Wishart, who was burned at the stake in 1546. Knox himself was punished for his involvement in the Reformation; one time arrested by the authorities and made a galley slave for 19 months.

But he became even more passionate in his desire for his nation's people to have a personal relationship with Christ. Knox prayed often, "Give me Scotland, or I die." When copies of Tyndale's translation of the Bible were smuggled into Scotland by merchants and read in secret, Knox encouraged home Bible study fellowships. People other than clergy seldom had copies of the Bible to read, and he wanted that changed.

His fiery sermons often contradicted the views of Queen Mary of Scots (Mary Stuart). She had him arrested and tried for treason in 1560, but he was acquitted. She once said, "I fear the prayers of John Knox more than all the armies of England."[7] By the time Knox died, the entire Scottish Parliament had adopted the Reformation.

Inside his residence are a few of his quotes. I liked this one: "When I think of those who have influenced my life the most, I think not of the great, but of the good." Another: "A man with God is always in the majority."

One biographer, commenting on his influence, wrote: "John Knox's shadow falls across the whole course of Scotland's religious development."[8] Talk about shadowing! Influencing!

Think back when you had an unexpected experience that surprised you. Or made you appreciate the simpler things in life. Maybe it was during a vacation. Or in a library. Or at work. Have yourself a great time remembering and then maybe go have some fun sharing the memory of the past.

Prayer: *Lord, thank You for those who went before us – the trailblazers – who encouraged others to read Your Word and to live up to its guidelines. Help me not to forget the sacrifice many made for the spread of Your message across the ages. Show me how to be more open to share Your goodness. Thank You, too, for memories associated with my past and for the ways You blessed me. In Jesus' name. Amen.*

Honoring the Military

Hate evil, love good, and establish justice in the gate! (Amos 5:15a NASB).

"[…] And this be our motto – 'In God is our trust'; And the star-spangled banner in triumph shall wave, O'er the land of the free, and the home of the brave."[9] – Francis Scott Key

I have a great respect for those who serve in the military, the defenders of freedom. Perhaps it goes back to my high school days during the Korean War. Many boys in our class who turned 18 joined the military branch of their choice rather than waiting to be drafted. Some left before they graduated. Many of us went to the train station to wave them off as they headed for basic training.

I went on to college but spent one summer in the Washington, D.C. area and was working for the Navy when armistice was signed and fighting ended on July 27, 1953. There I got a closer perspective on the horror of war, but a greater appreciation for those who help us keep our freedom.

I have listened to uncles, cousins, and even a brother relate personal war experiences. During World War II, one of my mother's cousins barely survived the long Bataan Death March in the Philippines during the spring of 1945. Thousands died during the march and imprisonment.[10]

Cousin Huey told me he survived because as an Alabama farm boy he had learned how to chew sugar cane, and while a prisoner he searched at night until he found cane along the death march. But he also said he had a strong will to live, while asking God for strength to survive. Personal accounts like these have touched my heart with gratitude for those who serve our country. Over the years as I've spoken on United States military bases both in this country and overseas, I have been able to thank a few of the soldiers.

I vividly remember one May first when I found myself in Japan on a U.S. base. We gathered around 50 American flags that snapped in the high wind. The occasion was the National Day of Prayer for America.

I was a visitor, just one in the crowd composed of members of a military band, choirs, school children, and servicemen and women with their families who met to pray for our nation. When we sang, "God bless America, land that I love," a knot formed in my throat in gratitude to God for my homeland and for the men and women stationed there.

As I approached the platform to give the history of the National Day of Prayer, I felt especially privileged to participate in this service – which because of the time zone was a day before they would observe this occasion in the U.S. mainland. The original base where we were, I was told, had been used by the Japanese pilots in World War II to train kamikaze pilots who would commit suicide to destroy their enemy. Now we stood on what was no longer enemy territory, praying for our own nation.

Sitting next to a serviceman on a plane some years ago, I thanked him for serving our country, and told him I pray for the military. "No one has ever told me that they pray for us. Please keep it up," he answered.

Prayer: *Lord, I pray for our military personnel and leaders in uniforms. Give them wisdom, knowledge, strength, and keen discernment for their tasks. Send angels to protect them and fight for all those upholding righteousness. I am deeply indebted to those who are dedicated to defending our country. Watch over their families and give them comfort and strength. Draw them all closer, still closer to You. Bless them I pray. In Jesus' name I pray. Amen.*

To Live Peaceful Lives

I urge, then, first of all, that petitions, prayers, intercession and thanksgiving be made for all people – for kings and all those in authority, that we may live peaceful and quiet lives in all godliness and holiness. This is good, and pleases God our Savior, who wants all men to be saved and to come to a knowledge of the truth (I Timothy 2:1-4).

"Liberty, when it begins to take root, is a plant of rapid growth." – George Washington

The song "America the Beautiful" was extremely popular during the difficult days of World War I, stirring patriotism and pride in our land. Though it was first printed in the *Boston Evening Transcript* on November 18, 1904, it had been originally composed in 1893 when a Massachusetts teacher, Kathrine Lee Bates, visited Colorado Springs. As she viewed the vastness of the land from atop nearby Pikes Peak, whose summit reaches 14,000 feet, she was so taken with the breathtaking view, she wrote a poem about its majesty. Sometime later a music composition by Samuel A. Ward was joined to Miss Bates' poem. The original poem underwent several revisions before its final rendition we know today.

> "O Beautiful for spacious skies
> For purple mountains majesties
> Above the fruited plain!
> America! America!
> God shed His grace on thee,
> And crown thy good with brotherhood
> From sea to shining sea." – Katherine Lee Bates (1893)

One biographer says that Miss Bates often remarked, "Unless we crown our good with brotherhood, of what lasting value are our spacious skies, our amber waves of grain, our mountain majesties, or our fruited plains?" Then she would add, "We must match the greatness of our country with the goodness of personal godly living."[11]

For 10 years I had a fantastic view of Pikes Peak from my upstairs home office windows. Often as I viewed the snowcapped mountain I thought about those words Miss Bates penned and I, too, asked God to shed His grace on our nation.

A few days after the infamous September 11, 2001 tragedy, with the loss of almost 3,000 Americans from terrorist attacks, I was driving down a busy street in Colorado Springs where people were clustered together singing. I was amazed as adults and children were loudly singing "America the Beautiful." Standing in the very shadow of Pikes Peak mountain, just ordinary Americans who loved their country were asking God's blessings on it through a song. I fought back tears.

I recalled an experience I had in Russia in the early 1990s, a few short years after the Soviet Union's communist regime collapsed. Along with 20 other Christian women from the United States, we were in Moscow after spending several weeks in other cities on a short-term mission trip. We had brought clothes for the orphanage we visited (two of our women later adopted several children), medical supplies for the pastor/doctor which our church doctors had donated, and Russian Bibles for pastors and students.

But on that final October Sunday morning as we stood in Red Square, we held a short, impromptu worship service. As far as I could tell we were the only ones around. Once hundreds of communist troops had displayed their strength by marching before Soviet leadership here to show off their weapons and military might.

I walked by myself over toward Lenin's now deserted mausoleum where crowds once stood in line to view him on his glass enclosed bier. Though this communist leader of the Bolshevik Revolution had died in 1924, he had been revered by many Russians for years afterwards.[12]

Moving as close as I could to the building holding his body, I lifted my Bible in my right hand and shouted, "Lenin is dead, but Jesus Christ is alive." For years Russia had been one of my "prayer burden" countries, and I was just one among millions of Christians world-wide who had prayed that the bondage to communism be broken here.[15] Now, years later when I recall that day, I am amazed at my boldness at shouting in Red Square. But I was grateful there were no longer soldiers patrolling the area to stop our group from worshiping our Lord.

Our memories are shadows that fall on us and stick with us throughout our lives. So when we need a smile, we can pull up the best ones and relish in the pleasure they bring. Some of mine include:

- In Seoul, Korea, attending services in a church which had the largest attendance in the world, and being awestruck at how beautiful the sound of praise and petitions offered in multi-languages before Almighty God sounded when the bell was rung for everyone to pray aloud at the same time. Then spending the next week out at Prayer Mountain, interceding with several hundred Christians from our country.

- In Buenos Aires, worshiping in a huge stadium with thousands while my good friend was the featured speaker.

- Sleeping on a mat on the floor in a Japanese home as a guest of a gracious host family.

- In Israel, being baptized in the River Jordan on a cold January first – a memorable New Year's Day.

- Standing on a chair in a Russian city, in a rented gymnasium room used for church services, I spoke through an interpreter – hoping that those standing in the packed hallway might also hear the message of Jesus' love for them.

- In Greece, standing on Mars Hill, trying to imagine what it was like when the Apostle Paul looked out from this spot to preach.

- In the Bavarian Alps mountain retreat area above Berchtesgaden, Germany, trying to finish writing a Christian magazine article on a borrowed hotel typewriter in the basement room where I was told Hitler had sometimes written his atrocious Nazi propaganda.

- In Florida, sitting in the backseat of a car interviewing a U.S. presidential candidate for a newspaper assignment, taking notes while he kindly held my tape recorder. Two secret service men in the front seat listened intently. The candidate was later elected President of the United States.

- Taking my 83-year-old granddaddy to watch the Apollo 14 space launch from the banks of the Indian River and hearing him yell, "Spectacular, spectacular!" Later at the Kennedy Space Center museum, I watched him gawk at the gray rock Neil Armstrong had brought back from his trip to the moon. Trying to comprehend this milestone, Granddaddy told me about his thrill at seeing his first automobile, a Model T Ford, over 60 years earlier. "What progress we've made," he said, shaking his head in wonder.

And now as a grandmother in my golden years, I wonder what wonders my descendants will experience.

I hope you have found, as I have, that happy memories are treasures to store. Maybe you can remember an event that touched you greatly. You close your eyes and smile and offer a silent prayer that you were part of something so simple, but so rewarding. You might begin by remembering certain events in your life or that of others when God displayed His miraculous power that left a lasting impression on you.

Memories can even offer a bit of clarity to our life's journey and can shadow us for years to come, even inspiring us in a good way.

Prayer: *Lord, thank You for our freedom, and for the many blessings You have heaped upon us. Thank You, too, for happy moments that give us happy memories. Unite us as a nation in heart and purpose to fulfill Your purpose for us. God, please shed Your grace on us, from sea to shining sea. I ask in Jesus' name that You would also work in my own life to help me achieve Your plan for me. Amen.*

Think on These Things

- Study Psalm 78 (see below) which begins with the following verses:

  My people, hear my teaching; listen to the words of my mouth. I will open my mouth with a parable; I will utter hidden things, things from of old — things we have heard and known, things our ancestors have told us. We will not hide them from their descendants; we will tell the next generation the praiseworthy deeds of the LORD, his power, and the wonders he has done (Psalm 78:1-4).

- Then make a list of memories or events that you would like to pass on to your children and their children and even the children yet to be born. One scripture to study: "This will be written for the generation to come, that a people yet to be created may praise the Lord" (Psalm 102:18 NKJV).

- Consider writing the memories in more detail or speaking into a recording device to save for them to share. Tell them of God's faithfulness to you; encourage them to follow the Lord themselves.

- Consider studying the following verses and think through how they might apply to you to pass on to your descendants: 1 Chronicles 16:14-17; Psalm 105:8-11; Isaiah 45:3-5; John 14: 23-25.

Part Thirteen

COMING FULL CIRCLE

Live in harmony with one another (Romans 12:16a).

"So if you want to unlock your hidden potential, spend your time with people who will stretch you. Find somebody who thinks faster, runs faster, and aims higher. Those are the people who will lift you up."[1] – John Maxwell

After a 20-year absence I was honored to be invited back to my former church as their women's retreat speaker – to the church where women had mentored me when I was a mom with three young children. I was asked to speak on "A House of Many Blessings," a topic of one of my books.

I realized I had come full circle – now I was a grandmother coming to encourage a younger generation of women who love the Lord.

At the last session, I spoke to the 300 in attendance on hospitality and mentoring, and paid tribute to some of the women from my past now seated at our roundtable. As I introduced each, I proudly acknowledged how each had influenced me those years gone by.

Mary Jo Looney had brought her decorating team to rearrange my home – moving furniture, hanging their newly made curtains, stapling sheets onto bedroom walls to match the bedspreads. Later on I was a part of her group by taking "before" and "after" photos of homes she decorated to give slide presentations to women's groups throughout the state – encouraging them to multiply this ministry of helps. She was the first one to encourage me to speak publicly in front of others at a Bible study.

Margaret, the most mature woman in our home group that met weekly at my house, had encouraged me in spiritual things, and had taught one of my daughters to bake bread and the other to become a better seamstress. In fact, when this daughter was a college freshman she decorated her dorm room in such unusual and beautiful ways that Margaret and Mary Jo had taught her that her teacher brought the entire Home Economics class to see it. After graduation, my daughter became a licensed interior decorator.

I introduced others at the luncheon. Lib, who had prayed faithfully with me on the phone for five minutes every weekday morning for 17 years. Liz, owner of a flower shop, had tried to teach me to make arrangements but was mostly my "let's have fun" pal who always made me laugh. Barbara, Louise, and Anne stood, and I mentioned others unable to be there, listing their giftings which had figured heavily in my growth – casting their shadows on my life as an influencer. I thanked them all and sat down to eat lunch.

We had just started on our dessert when a young woman came to our table and asked if she could address us "older" women. She said those sitting at her table in the back corner were from a church in another city. Yet they had made an important decision just now. We urged her to tell us.

She explained: "When those of us heard how you have been friends all these years – even when one moved away – and how you have continued to pray for one another, we were touched. We made a commitment today to do the same. We want to keep lifelong friendships like you have had, and we want to pray for each other, too. Thank you for a great show-and-tell lesson."[2] Most of us "oldies" choked back a tear. "They caught what we taught," Mary Jo said with a smile.

Some years later, when Mary Jo had turned 90, I travelled 450 miles to visit her. I had truly come full circle now, sitting once again at her feet listening to wisdom as she talked. And I learned she was still mentoring younger women who came to her house.

The next year when the call came that she had left this earth, I smiled remembering all the ways she had touched my life. For more than 30 years she had called me on my birthday and had mailed me a card with a two-dollar bill tucked inside. I have an envelope full of those dollars. What's more, she did the same for those other women she had mentored. What an influencer. What a shadow she cast over me.

Prayer: *Thank You, O Lord, for those You bring into our lives to encourage and teach us in such practical ways. Thanks for the individuals who recognize the* *hidden potential in us and help us achieve things we never dreamed we could accomplish. Amen.*

Dream with No Regrets

And now, Lord, what do I wait for and expect? My hope and expectation are in You (Psalm 39:7 AMPC).

"Twenty years from now you will be more disappointed by the things you didn't do than by the things you did do. So throw off the bowlines. Sail away from the safe harbor, catch the winds in your sail. Explore – dream and discover."
– Mark Twain

Dream versus goal:

"A dream is a hope of a positive expectation for sometime in the future. A goal is a dream with a timetable associated with it." – Anonymous

Going by that broad definition, why not dream for the future by setting some realistic, workable goals to help achieve that dream?

First, schedule time for some creative dreaming. Let your imagination go and come up with various possibilities – even those you have never previously considered. Ask God to give you inspired, innovative ideas to ponder. Ask the Holy Spirit for divine guidance then for practical goals to achieve them.

Sooner or later this will lead to you asking Him for some divine-ordained assignments. Don't give in to fear. Fear, it has been said, kills more dreams than failure. Grab hold of faith! You can do it – with His help.

Here is a quote from Jamie Buckingham I've kept in my notebook for many years.

> In Van Dyke's "The Other Wise Man," Artaban was advised to go on the quest for the promised king. He was warned, however, that it would be a long hard pilgrimage and possibly prove to be an empty search. "But," he said, "*it is better to follow even the shadow of the best than to remain content with the worst*" (author's italics).
>
> I wonder if there is anybody left, willing to dream the impossible dream and let their shadow fall on others?[3]

Dutch Sheets reminds us, "Your Designer dreamed dreams for you before you were even born, then skillfully wove them into your DNA as you were created, along with the ability to find and fulfill them. His destiny for you will be the sum of those dreams. The journey of life, then, is meant to be a dream quest; finding what your Maker has dreamed for you brings life's ultimate satisfaction and should be life's ultimate pursuit."[4]

Prayer: *Lord, prepare me for what You have prepared for me! Amen.*

When You Need God's Love

[T]hey were at their wits' end. Then they cried out to the LORD in their trouble, and he brought them out of their distress (Psalm 107: 27b, 28).

What a Friend We Have in Jesus

Can we find a friend so faithful,

Who will all our sorrows share?

Jesus knows our every weakness –

Take it to the Lord in prayer…

In His arms He'll take and shield you,

You will find a solace there. Amen.

– Joseph Scriven (1820-1886)

Stormy times come into our lives – unsettling times when we must seek the Lord on our own and let His shadow and His voice be our comfort. For me it happened one winter afternoon in a cemetery.

I spread a green blanket over my husband's grave and plopped down on it. Opening my small Bible, I began to read it aloud. I was not here to communicate with my husband – I knew that was wrong – but rather to have a talk with the Lord. To reassure myself of His promises for me, now that He was my husband. To try to hear His voice for my future.

Christmas, just three days away, would mark my wedding anniversary. This year I was planning no celebration. My husband had gone to heaven some weeks earlier. Today I made the 40-minute drive to deliver a red poinsettia to the grave in the far eastern corner of the cemetery. Here by my husband were the burial sites of my mother, two aunts, and the uncle who gave me away at my wedding. A police station was next door, separated only by a chain link fence.

The breeze off the Gulf of Mexico, just a few blocks away, almost drowned out my voice as I began to quote Psalm 23, "The Lord is my Shepherd, I shall not want."

Then personalizing Psalm 121, I yelled into the wind, "The Lord is my Keeper. The Lord will protect me from all evil; He will keep my soul; He will guard my going out and my coming in forever." Six times, that Psalm repeats *keeps* or *preserves*, meaning God is my caregiver.

As other promises leapt into my heart, I proclaimed them even louder: "The Lord is my Provider. He will meet all my needs, according to His riches in glory… The Lord is my Comforter…"

For the next 30 minutes as tears spilled onto my blanket, I shouted various Scriptures. Policemen came and went, getting in and out of their patrol cars. I didn't care if they heard me. I decreed comforting Psalms, warfare Scriptures, prophetic verses – all the while letting God's precious Word minister to my heart.

The Lord seemed to whisper to me, "What do you see?"

Looking around, I observed acres of gravesites and realized I was alone in the cemetery. Before I could respond to His question, His voice came again. "Yes, everyone here in this place is dead. You are the only one alive. So, get up and act alive!"

His direction startled me. "Get up and act alive." Yes, that's what I had come to hear. My watershed moment, my turning-around point, had come to me in a cemetery. I would go home and celebrate my anniversary with some of my children and grandchildren on Christmas Day.

The Lord is indeed my keeper! His keeping power will sustain me. I will act alive. I am alive. I choose to let God impart hope and guide me on this difficult new journey.[5]

What about you? Are you going through a heartbreaking crisis? Have you got a desperate need that you need to speak to God about? A difficult circumstance? A great loss? A sense of hopelessness? Like the Psalmist, do you feel like you are at your wit's end, too?

Maybe now is a good time to pause and ask God to speak personally to you. His Word promises that He still has plans for you, plans for you to prosper, plans to give you a hope and a future (Jeremiah 29:11). I have been a widow some years now and I can attest to His faithfulness.

One day I wrote this in my journal for my own encouragement. Maybe you can identify.

I cannot see around the bend, but He is there. In my 'unknown' to me, is His purpose, plan, destiny, yes, even His guidance to the right path. His help, His comfort, His shining Light inviting me to gather near and follow in His shadow. What's around the corner, the bend, Lord? I do not know. Cannot even guess. Show me clearly. Lead me. I will bless the Lord and not forget all His benefits. Now I will read Psalm 103 and began to list His benefits.

Remember, whatever you are going through – know that He cares.

Prayer: *Heavenly Father, please help me to adjust to new experiences, ones which I must now walk through. Guide me and don't let me miss Your plan for* *my life. Now, show me what it is You have for me to do! Help me to act alive and be fully alive, expectant for You to intervene and see me through, Lord. Help me. Amen.*

Living Our Dash Well

I have fought the good fight, I have finished the race, I have kept the faith. Now there is in store for me the crown of righteousness, which the Lord, the righteous Judge, will award to me on that day – and not only to me, but also to all who have longed for his appearing (2 Timothy 4:7-8).

"Be kind to your shadow." – Rebecca Lawless

Most gravestones have a dash between the birthday and the death of the person buried there. Linda Ellis wrote a poem called "The Dash," challenging us to live our lives well between the dash – from our birth to our death. She asks when our eulogy is being read with our "life's actions to rehash," would we be proud of how we spent our dash?[6]

Not far from my husband's gravesite is a monument for a young woman that reads: "She Lived Her Dash Well." Wow, I wish I had known her. One husband and wife's headstone says, "We Had Fun." Doesn't it make you curious about their happy lives? Let me tell you about a friend of mine whose obituary in the local newspaper makes me laugh with joy every time I reread it.

Dolores lived in a little town about 20 miles from me. A town with one traffic light, one grocery store, one gas station, and a few businesses, including hers. Friends dropped in often for coffee and sometimes when several showed up at the same time we'd have a full-fledged prayer meeting. She was the chief prayer warrior.

Her obituary in the newspaper expressed her life boldly. It began with her name, followed by the dates 1930-2008 and a statement: *On a glorious blue sky afternoon on April 16, the Heavens in indescribable majesty welcomed Dolores…* Then it told about her family who had preceded her in death and listed some of her accomplishments as a business owner in her small community. It ended with this:

> The Lord blessed Dolores with His heart. She was quick to give if you were in need. Should you whisper to her 'pray for me' in Kelly's [grocery store], be prepared for an out-loud, Pentecostal, hell-shaking, hallelujah response right there between the Jim Dandy grits and the black-eyed peas. The world has lost another warrior of righteousness, and Heaven has received another faithful servant. She will be sorely missed.[7]

I hope it made you smile, too. My dash is still being lived out, my race still being run. I hope when mine is over that my headstone can read, "She Finished the Race Well." Isn't that your desire, too?

Prayer: *Lord, give us divine opportunities and occasions to help others succeed – to make positive and significant deposits into other people's lives. Help us run well Your race for us. Amen.*

Watch Over Your Sphere of Influence

Laboring together [as God's fellow workers] with Him then, we beg of you not to receive the grace of God in vain [that merciful kindness by which God exerts His holy influence on souls and turns them to Christ, keeping and strengthening them – do not receive it to no purpose] (2 Corinthians 6:1 AMPC).

"Keep watch over your field, your vineyard, your family, your church, your health, your money, your faith – all the things you are responsible for. You are the tenant manager. But never forget who owns the field."[8] – Jamie Buckingham.

Buckingham continued:

"You may not think your little field is very important. But God has set you in your field as a watchman. Each one of us has a sphere of influence. Most of us don't realize it, but our influence is much larger than we can ever imagine – and will continue on for generations to come, be it good or evil. It's a wonderful responsibility – frightening at times – but wonderful. Always remember, though, you're never in your watchtower alone. Jesus is ever with you, and His Spirit will whisper just the things you need to say and do."[9]

In this book, *Cast Your Shadow: Influence On Purpose*, we have come full circle. Let's recall a quote from Part One in which Jamie Buckingham spoke:

"You look back across your life and you will remember numbers of people who have let their shadow fall on you. Because of that you are who you are today. I want to encourage you. Your shadow perhaps unbeknownst to you is falling on a number of other people. God is healing and God is blessing [...] because your face is toward Jesus. Ordinary people doing extraordinary things through God for God."

Each of us can take the challenge to cast a bigger shadow on more people. Let's go do it. Let's make a difference. Let's expand our territory. Let's use our talents and experience to help shape the destiny of others. And in the process thank God for the blessing it is to us.

Prayer: *Father, I thank You for those who have let me come under their shadow. Bless them for their contribution to my life. I thank You, too, for those who have let me have the honor to influence and impart something special to them. May each of us fulfill Your destiny for us and continue to be laborers in Your field. To You be the glory. Amen.*

Think On These Things

Dare to dream:

- What are your dreams?
- What are your goals?
- What do you need to do to get there?
- Who are the people to help you achieve this goal?

- What changes, if there are any, do you need to make to achieve it? Take classes? Switch locations or job? Become more disciplined?

- Who are people you can learn from?

- Who are the people you can reach?

- Who are the influencers in your life?

- Who are you influencing?

- Who could you be influencing?

- What is the first thing you tell yourself when you wake each morning? Little Piglet told his friend Winnie the Pooh Bear his first thoughts to himself: "I wonder what's going to happen exciting today?" Can we, too, look for exciting things in each day? Why not? Jesus came to give us life, life abundant. And that is an exciting promise.

APPENDIX A

Are you ready to ponder these questions more thoroughly, using some "thinking" time to jot down ways other people or things have blessed you? Also recall ways you were instrumental in the life of others. Then offer thanks to God for the priceless occasions! Here are some questions to ponder:

1. Who were the people whose shadow you deliberately moved under? You let them influence you – mentor, encourage, correct, or advise you. And your life was enriched. What lessons did you learn? What lasting words of encouragement do you cherish? Did you thank them?

2. Who were the "influencers" in your life but they never knew? Perhaps you were inspired or encouraged by something they did, said, or wrote. Thank God for their influence in your life.

3. Who were those you influenced on purpose? You chose to speak into their lives. Maybe you taught them a skill. Or perhaps you just enjoyed sharing food, fun, and fellowship. But you invested time in them.

4. Do you know how or if your shadow, unbeknownst to you, fell on someone when you were doing just what you knew to do, whether in daily activity, volunteering, or going the extra mile to offer aid? Yet God helped you be His hands extended? Just think, God Himself is our rewarder (See Ruth 2:12).

5. Who were historical figures you never knew but whose lives or acts of heroism influenced you? Who were the somebodies who wrote a book, painted a picture, composed music, produced a movie, passed a congressional bill, or did something so impressive you have used those actions as a role model? Are you going to share their story with others?

The One Anothers

Reciprocal Living: "one another" and "each other" are reciprocal pronouns, meaning that two or more people act equally to one another. Here are some of the commands for that.

Love one another. (John 13:34; Romans 13:8)

Depend on one another. (Romans 12:4, 5)

Be devoted to one another. (Romans 12:10)

Wash each other's feet. (John 13:14)

Rejoice with one another. (Romans 12:15; 1 Corinthians 12:26)

Weep with one another. (Romans 12:15)

Live in harmony with one another. (Romans 12:16)

Don't judge one another. (Romans 14:13)

Accept one another. (Romans 15:7)

Admonish one another. (Colossians 3:16)

Greet one another. (Romans 16:16)

Wait for one another. (1 Corinthians 11:33)

Care for one another. (1 Corinthians 12:25)

Serve one another. (Galatians 5:13)

Be kind to one another. (Ephesians 4:32)

Forgive one another. (Ephesians 4:32)

Be compassionate toward one another. (Ephesians 4:32)

Encourage one another. (1 Thessalonians 5:11; Hebrews 10:25)

Submit to one another. (Ephesians 5:21)

Bear with one another. (Ephesians 4:2)

Stimulate one another to love and good deeds. (Hebrews 10:24)

Be hospitable to one another without complaint. (1 Peter 4:9)

Minister to one another with your gifts. (1 Peter 4:10)

Be sensitive to one another, clothed in humility. (1 Peter 5:5)

Do not speak evil of one another. (James 4:11)

Do not grumble against one another. (James 5:9)

Confess your sins to one another. (James 5:16)

Pray for one another. (James 5:16)

Fellowship with one another. (1 John 1:7)

Do not become arrogant against one another. (1 Corinthians 4:6)

Carry one another's burdens. (Galatians 6:2)

Give preference to one another in honor. (Romans 12:10)

Instruct and counsel one another. (Romans 15:14)

Comfort one another. (2 Corinthians 1:4)

Contribute to the needs of the saints. (Romans 12:13)

Scriptures for Shadow

The apostles performed many miraculous signs and wonders among the people. [...] Nevertheless, more and more men and women believed in the Lord and were added to their number. As a result, people brought the sick to the streets and laid them on beds and mats so that at least Peter's shadow might fall on some of them as he passed by. Crowds gathered also from the towns around Jerusalem, bringing their sick and those tormented by impure spirits, and all of them were healed (Acts 5:12a, 14-16).

Every good and perfect gift is from above, coming down from the Father of the heavenly lights, who does not change like shifting shadows (James 1:17).

Keep me as the apple of your eye; hide me in the shadow of your wings (Psalm 17:8).

How priceless is your unfailing love, O God! People take refuge in the shadow of your wings (Psalm 36:7).

Because you are my help, I sing in the shadow of your wings (Psalm 63:7).

Whoever dwells in the shelter of the Most High will rest in the shadow of the Almighty. I will say of the Lord, "He is my refuge and my fortress, my God, in whom I trust." [...] [U]nder his wings you will find refuge (Psalm 91:1, 2, 4b).

Scriptures for Overshadowed

Matthew 17:1-8

Mark 9:7

Luke 9:34

Luke 1:35

Praying The Alphabet, Worshiping God

You are worthy, our Lord and God, to receive glory and honor and power, for You created all things, and by Your will they were created and have their being (Revelation 4:11).

We can help our todays and tomorrows go smoother by worshiping our Lord and agreeing with His written Word. With the living creatures in heaven we can say God is worthy to receive glory and honor and power.

Often during my quiet time in prayer, I go through the alphabet and concentrate on the characteristics of the Trinity – our Heavenly Father's greatness; Jesus, His Son's love to die for our sins; and the Holy Spirit, our Comforter and Teacher. Then I add my praise and thanks aloud, naming things about whom the Godhead is and why I am grateful. You can add others to this list:

A: Almighty God, Abba Father, Ancient of Days, Awesome God, Alpha and Omega.
B: Bread of Life, Bright and Morning Star, Balm of Gilead, Blood of the Lamb, Blessing and honor and glory and power are due Your name.
C: Christ, Covenant Keeper, Comforter.
D: Divine, Deliverer, Destroyer of Sin.
E. Eternal, Everlasting God, Excellent, Exalted, Encourager.
F: Father, Faithful Friend, Forgiver, Faultless, Fortress.
G: Good Shepherd, God of Glory, Grace, Giver of Life.
H: Holy One, Holy Spirit, High Priest, Healer, Helper, Hope.
I: Immanuel, I AM, Indescribable, Immortal, Invisible.
J: Jehovah, Jesus, Just Judge.
K: King of kings, Keeper.
L: Lord of lords, Lamb of God, Lord God Almighty, Living Word, Light of the World, Lord of hosts, Lion of Judah.
M: Master, Maker of heaven and earth, Messiah, Mediator, Magnificent, Majestic.
N: Name above all names, Nazarene, New mercies every morning.
O: Omnipotent, Omnipresent, Only Begotten, Omega.
P: Prince of Peace, Provider, Potter, Protector, Praiseworthy.
Q: Quieter of my storms, Quite a Provider, Quenches my thirst.

R: Redeemer, Righteous, Repairer of the Breach, Restorer, Rock of Salvation.

S: Savior, Shepherd, Son of God, Son of Man.

T: Truth, Teacher, Transformer, Trustworthy, Triumphant.

U: Understanding, Universal, Upright.

V: Victorious, Vine, Virtuous, Voice of God.

W: Warrior, Worthy, Wise, Who is and Who was and Who is to come, the Word.

X: EXtra-ordinary in all Your ways.

Y: Yahweh (Hebrew name for God).

Z: Zealous – "He will arouse His zeal like a man of war. […] He will prevail against His enemies" (Isaiah 42:13 NASB).[1]

APPENDIX B

And the Shadow Spread

People Who Say Quin's Shadow Touched Them

My life was forever changed when Quin Sherrer's shadow fell across my life. In truth, it may not have gracefully fallen on me, it may have knocked me over. And, all for the good. It has now been over 30 years and she continues to touch my life deeply. I know of no other woman who has encouraged me, believed in me, and spoken truth into my life in such a powerful way. Her desire to see not only me, but others, grow into all God has for you is unparalleled. In fact, I have a "keeper" file with notes I go back to for hope, direction, and reminders of God's love and direction. I would say 90 percent of that file bears her name.

I have always considered one of God's most precious ways to show His love is through the quality people He puts in our lives. He has loved me big through Quin. We have laughed, cried, prayed, and grown together. Only eternity will tell how grateful I am for this mighty force in the Kingdom of God and the powerful way her life has indeed graced mine! She is Mama Quin to me and holds a prized place in my heart. – **JoNell Gerland**, President, Treasure in Clay International, Houston, Texas

I remember the day Quin walked through our doors at Victory Christian Fellowship in Somerset, Kentucky. She unlocked a world that we didn't know existed through her book *A Women's Guide to Spiritual Warfare*. I'm so grateful our relationship continued from there. She has continually been a mentor to me and my family, being only a phone call or e-mail away. Mentoring is not something you can Google. It requires human dialogue. Quin, you've not just impacted me, but you are mentoring the generation after me. Heaven will be richer because of it. Thank you, friend. – **Mrs. Jeanette Harrell**, Pastor's wife, Victory Christian Fellowship, Somerset, Kentucky

Quin: Your influence in my life is unmistakable. Not only have you inspired me as a writer, as I have been mentored by you, but your prayer life has affected me as well. You have stood as Shammah in 2 Samuel and held your ground and fought for your family and others God added to your "bean patch." You have been a treasure in my life. Thank you. – **Sherry Anderson**, Author, College Writing Instructor, Panama City, Florida

Quin's shadow was cast over my life some 30 years ago when a mutual friend invited me to a prayer retreat where she was speaking. Before the weekend was over she asked me to work with her on a book project she wanted help with in order to meet the publisher's deadline. That led to our co-writing 19 books together over the years following, including our bestseller, *A Woman's Guide to Spiritual Warfare*. I'm so grateful for Quin's friendship, her prayer support, and all the blessings God has poured into my life through her shadow!
– **Ruthanne Garlock**, Author, Chairman, Garlock Ministry, Bulverde, Texas

I was a young mom, and in my early 30s, when I met Quin. I was new to the things of the Spirit and had been crying out to the Lord for someone to mentor me. I will never forget when I was first exposed to Quin's teaching; it was in 1999 at the Woman of Destiny conference in Van Nuys, California. It was as if the Lord was showing me, through Quin's message, what a life led by the Spirit could look like. The following year, I invited Quin to minister at our very evangelical church. Quin was brilliant in how she created a bridge between the world of evangelicals and the world of charismatics. It was as if the Word was married to Power that day, and my church was forever changed as people accepted the invitation to walk in an ever deepening relationship with the Lord.

Over the years, she and I have continued to stay in contact via telephone, e-mail, and conferences, and she has continued to "cast

her shadow" upon me and train me up in the things of the Lord. She has challenged me to begin, with intentionality, to cast my own shadow upon others. I have been doing that for almost 20 years now. The Lord has used me to mentor significant leaders and influencers in both the church and in the marketplace, both nationally and internationally. I challenge them in the same way Quin continues to challenge me, to "cast their shadow" upon others. Many of the individuals I meet with are in significant roles of influence, and the shadow they cast for Jesus to see the Kingdom of God advance is huge. Countless lives have been touched. I can trace all of this back to that day when God answered my prayer for a mentor and brought Quin into my life. I am eternally grateful to Him for Mama Quin!
– **Christina Horn**, President, Shift Ministries, Alta Loma, California

In the 30 plus years I've known Quin I have profited much following the example she lived in front of me. I seldom missed an opportunity to hear her speak at Aglow meetings or retreats and have avidly read all her books. However, the life changing shadow that touched my life came about through observing the practical way she applied Christianity to her everyday life. She taught me to pray Scripture and to listen to how others prayed. Once I was driving her to speak at a retreat in Austin, Texas when she began to pray out loud, speaking to Jesus so directly and personally I would not have been surprised if I'd seen His face in my rearview mirror.

Quin opens her home, where ever she lives, and it is always warm and loving. Never is there any doubt Jesus is the guest of honor. That was certainly true in her small apartment on Christ For The Nations Institute campus in Dallas where students crammed in to share her meals after Sunday services, with two of my children among them. I am so blessed knowing my picture is on her prayer board along with the others she prays for regularly. The shadow she cast on me is the gift that causes me to follow after the One I know she pursues – our Savior. – **Charlene Strock**, Wife of retired Air Force officer, Dripping Springs, Texas

Quin: Thank you for your obedience to the Holy Spirit. You have definitely cast a shadow of wisdom in my life on more than one occasion! The first time was through your book *A Woman's Guide to Breaking Bondages*. That led to your doing a women's retreat for me at

Waukaway Springs, Mississippi. Your influence expanded my bean patch of prayer and my prayer walking in my neighborhood. You then used my prayer partner testimony in one of your books. Most recently your influence had to do with our transition to Birmingham. God used you to encourage me to press in, and trust God completely with the sale of our North Carolina home. You gave me scriptures to use and encouraged me to pray for the family who needed our house. And a few weeks later we got a cash offer. Praise Jesus. – **Cynthia Duke**, Businesswoman, Pelham, Alabama

While attending a national conference for Protestant Women of the Chapel in Colorado Springs in 1996, I heard Quin speak about the importance of taking care of our home and creating an environment that reinforces our relationship with Christ. She exuded a confidence and authority which created a hunger in me. Several years later, while serving as the international president of Protestant Women of the Chapel, I saw her once again at one of our regional conferences where we were both speakers. Quin encouraged me to keep sharing my story wherever I could. We stayed in touch and she always encouraged me to keep moving forward with my leadership of others. Today, I am an ordained minister, who speaks at women's gatherings and have established a prayer network of women associated with the military to help equip them in their gifts and callings and encourage them to go deep with God in an intimate relationship. My husband and I speak at marriage retreats and go on the road to pray and establish God's purposes whenever we can.

Through Quin's example and mentoring, her shadow drew me into a deeper relationship with Jesus. She has fanned the flames of the gifts of God in me and now I am boldly sharing the gospel of Jesus Christ and the work of the Holy Spirit. I am ripe fruit from her ministry. For that and more, I am eternally grateful for her investment in my life and am passing it on to another generation. – **Brenda Marlin**, Former International President, Protestant Women of the Chapel International, Whitesboro, Texas

Many years ago after reading Quin's first book, *How to Pray for Your Children*, a friend and I in Lexington started a prayer group to do just that – pray for our children weekly. Soon our husbands joined us on Wednesday nights in our home. There were 17 of us in the original group. After all these years we still meet when needed. It really helped that Quin came periodically to our home in Kentucky to encourage us. And she still keeps up with us now through e-mail and telephone. Our dependence on God carried us through the child rearing years and established long time, loving relationships among our praying parents. When out-of-town friends learned how we were praying for our children, using Quin's book as our guide, they asked some of us to come help them start "Praying for Your Children" groups too. Out of that beginning group here in Lexington, several of our daughters later started their own prayer groups. God keeps blessing. – **Dorothea Sims**, Former Area Aglow Officer, Lexington, Kentucky

I have had the honor and blessing of having Quin Sherrer in my life. Our friendship developed because my mother and Quin were prayer partners. Our families became connected, as God often orchestrates. I'm so thankful for the late night sleepovers at the beach we have had when my family vacationed near where she lived in Florida. Also for the spontaneous prayer meetings we've had, our church's women's retreat where she taught, and the wisdom Quin has shared with me and my family over many years. I've been so blessed to have Quin's shadow fall in such a personal way. She is a spiritual mother, a teacher, and friend to me! I love her! – **Tracey Gregory**, Radio host, Mother of three, Milan, Tennessee

I am so thankful for my dear friend, Quin! Her gift of encouragement has meant so much to me over the years. No matter what has happened, she always has found a way to be positive and uplifting. She validates people, though they may be young and inexperienced in the things of God. Even in times when I felt I had messed up, her words have brought life into my sagging spirit. I love that she will take time to sit down with me and let me share whatever is on my mind and then encourage me with her wisdom and understanding. She has been a major source of encouragement to me, and I am so thankful that God brought her into my life more than 35 years ago. – **Mary Beth Pichotta**, Retired RN, Milford, Connecticut

I was a former school teacher, wife of an Air Force officer, and mother of two sons years ago when I got a copy of Quin's book *How to Pray for Your Children* while we were stationed in England. It transformed the way I prayed for my children and other children. She provided a practical guide to prayer, and it led the way to many breakthroughs and answered prayers. She helped me to understand the authority and power our prayers have and to be bold. She also gave me strategies for many special needs. For 27 years I have read Quin's books, and they have been life changing for me and my family. I have then shared teachings from them with others. She is an accomplished speaker, and we are fortunate to have her speak for our local Mothers of Preschoolers group. I have learned more about prayer from Quin's books than from any other person. – **Jane Davis**, Elder, Generations United Church, A Mentor Mom, Niceville, Florida

The Holy Spirit constantly wields Quin's teaching like a power sword to help me pray through battles and trials. When my prayer mentor first introduced me to Quin, she was teaching on intercessory prayer. I was a young mom with a 2-year-old and struggled with tremendous insecurity about my parenting abilities. I purchased her book *A Mother's Guide to Praying for Your Children*. Those teachings and testimonies changed my entire trajectory in raising my kids! Later, I picked up Quin's book *A Woman's Guide to Spiritual Warfare*. Several times the Holy Spirit sent me to specific page numbers in her book that spoke to my exact situations!

My prayer partner and I were marveling yesterday about the way God is using the ripple effect of Quin's books and teachings. Just the fact that I have a prayer partner in the first place is Quin's influence! Many women in our lives are now equipped to pray through what we've learned from Quin and our well-worn, dog-eared copies of her books.

I praise God for Quin – for her strength and prayerfulness, her faith and vigor. She never gives up and never backs down. – **Danita Jenae**, Florida, Writer/Poet/Artist: *SplatterJoy.com*

Quin calls me her "laughing friend" which is a compliment because she phones me long distance when she needs a good laugh. Many years ago when our husbands were among the early aerospace engineers at Kennedy Space Center, I prayed for my husband, Jim, to have a close male friend. The answer came with Quin's husband,

LeRoy. They had a close work relationship and since both loved to fly they soon enjoyed hours together in our four-seated Cherokee Arrow 200 plane. Quin and I then became close buddies. She was a busy mother, a reporter for our local newspaper, and wrote booklets for our church. I call her my "study the Bible" friend as she often shares Scripture nuggets with me from her very marked up Bible. When she comes back to visit our town where her family lived almost 20 years, she always stays with me. While finishing this book she came to our church to speak to the Widow's Walk group and to the women attending our retreat. I saw how her shadow had fallen not only on me but on many women who came to talk to her and relate various incidents where her writings or her life had impacted them.
– **Elizabeth Graham**, Retired decorator and business owner, Titusville, Florida

Love this new book! I am a long-time fan of Quin Sherrer's books. I have used them regularly as a research resource as I taught on prayer in my Sunday School classes and Bible Studies. I have also gladly given them as gifts. When I found out that she had written a new book and saw the title, *Cast Your Shadow: Influence on Purpose*, I was privileged to read her first draft. It's a most personal, touching book as Quin shares with her readers the people and experiences that have influenced her during her life – from pastors, other authors and journalists, her church families, next door neighbors, people on airlines, prayer partners far and wide, and her many readers. I enjoyed reading about them all and how many of them impacted her life. This book served as a reminder that I am casting my shadow, influencing others, and will be leaving a legacy. – **Kate Buchanan**, Businesswoman, Tallahassee, Florida

It was the last class. I was about to complete an 18-month Ministry Leadership Intensive school designed to equip and impart leaders for ministry – home, marketplace, global, or church – wherever God planted you. I walked into this class with only one prayer, "Lord, please tell me what you want me to do next."

I had no idea He was about to answer that prayer through a petite fireball, full of the Spirit of God, overflowing with wisdom, humor, prayer, and partnership – Quin Sherrer. Now 14 years later, I look back and see the shadow Quin cast over me. From the early days of driving her to speaking engagements…oh, those long lingering car conversations. They began to draw a clearer picture of who I was in ministry.

Quin didn't just write about prayer or teach about prayer. This woman prays. She prayed instant prayers, powerful prayers, prophetic prayers. She awakened prayer in me like never before. She didn't just talk about mentoring. She mentored. She became a spiritual mother who gave me the courage to serve God out of my comfort zone. She didn't just profess the Scriptures. Quin showed me how to live strong in faith, persevering in troubled times, overcoming life's tests and challenges and heartaches.

I had no idea God's plans were for me to join a young church and help develop a culture of prayer that has grown to a multi-campus world-wide ministry. I had no idea I would travel the nations and teach prayer. I had no idea I would author books. God did. Everyone needs someone further ahead calling them higher. I am eternally grateful God answered my wanting prayer with more than I knew I would need – a Quin willing and more than able to cast a long shadow for me. - **Mary Jo Pierce**, Pastor of Prayer and Intercession, Gateway Church, Dallas-Ft. Worth Metroplex

I have known Quin for more than 30 years, and now I am writing about this 30th book of hers. How extraordinary! It is amazing to me to read this special book that is needed now, when people everywhere need help and hope. To cast our shadow seems a most important thing for us to do in such a stressed-filled world.

I love the story in Part One about pastor and writer Jamie Buckingham who was a friend of mine. He did not know he was casting his shadow over the Aborigines, so I love it that our shadow goes on, even when we don't know it.

This book affected me in three ways. 1. This book started me on some studying, notes, and Scriptures in the Appendix in the back of the book. 2. Then Quin's well-done Part Twelve, which includes wisdom from our leaders of the past, challenged me to look more earnestly around me for those who need help. 3. This book reminded me of past memories that I should write down for my grandchildren. Even those chance encounters such as Quin writes about brought back memories I should share. This book is full of treasures. **– Sally Britt**, Birmingham, AL

Endorsements for Other Books Quin Sherrer Has Written or Co-Authored

Foreword: *Hope for a Widow's Heart: Encouraging Reflections for Your Journey*

Quin and I go back many years, We served the Lord together in the ministry of Aglow from Quin's early days as a local officer to each level of leadership in which she has served, including the national leadership for the ministry in the United States. I've had the joy of being the recipient of her caring friendship as we have co-labored together through the years.

A well-loved writer, speaker, and encourager, Quin is a respected woman of God throughout Aglow and the body of Christ. Her prolific pen has produced an impressive body of work, with many bestsellers related to the subject of prayer. Her books have impacted countless lives around the world with their truth and practical applications for everyday living.

This book [*Hope for a Widow's Heart*] sprang from Quin's own transition from wife to widow. She weaves together real-life stories from women who grappled with an often unwanted and unexpected life experience. And with powerful scriptures from the Word of God, Quin offers help and hope to those on their journey of grief…Take Quin's hand as she leads you on this pathway from grief to hope, from darkness to light and sadness to new joy. You will find her a warm and comforting companion on your journey. – **Jane Hansen Hoyt**, President/CEO Aglow International, Edmonds, Washington

Endorsements: *Hope for a Widow's Heart*

Quin Sherrer is the kind of person with whom others feel comfortable sharing their struggles. A widow herself, she relates her own journey and those of widows young and old, in a wide variety of circumstances, through the hardest of passages. It is all here: the confusion, the near unbearable pain, the mistakes, but also the hard-worn wisdom and surprising renewal. This is a rare book: unflinching about the darkness, but rich in hope. – **Elizabeth Sherrill**, Author, *All the Way to Heaven* and Co-author, *The Hiding Place* (for Corrie ten Boom)

No matter what "stage of widowhood" you are in, this book will benefit you. It has been ten years since I watched my husband die on that mountain in the Philippine jungle, but I found this book full of wise words just for me! You will learn from women who have been there. – **Gracia Burnham**, Author of the bestseller *In The Presence of Mine Enemies*

When Quin and I lived in the same city, we met regularly to pray for our families. Now that she has entered a new season, she has written this hope-filled book with appropriate prayers, as well as biblical, practical insights to encourage other widows. I highly recommend *Hope for a Widow's Heart*. – **Mrs. Dick (Dee) Eastman**, Every Home for Christ, Colorado Springs, Colorado

Almost every day I visit people who have lost a partner. I know of no greater pain in this life. Sorrow is inevitable, but as Christians we do not have to sorrow without hope. Not only has Quin been through such a time, but she is a very blessed writer, able to put into simple, practical terms great helps for those experiencing this pain. As a long-term pastor of Quin and LeRoy and having met with them in a small group once a week for six years, I deeply appreciated their commitment to our Lord Jesus Christ. *Hope for a Widow's Heart* will not only bring you comfort and hope, but it is a book you can use to minister to others. – **Rev. Peter Lord**, Pastor Emeritus, Park Avenue Baptist Church, Titusville, Florida, Author of *The 2959 Plan: A Guide to Communion with God*.

Foreword: *Listen, God Is Speaking to You*

It is a tremendous honor to write a foreword for one of Quin's books [*Listen, God Is Speaking to You*]. When you hold someone in the place of esteem in which I hold Quin, the honor is profound. This book is for those who would be wise; those who believe God speaks and who desire to hear Him. It is also for those who want to believe He speaks but aren't sure; for after reading it, your hope will be satisfied, your fears allayed: God does, indeed, still speak today.

With artistic skill, using real life stories as the paint and the ways and Word of God as the brush, Quin gives us more than words – she gives us the painting. Some, like Quin, simply have that rare ability to paint with words. This book will draw you closer to the Father which should be the litmus test of any Christian book, and enable you to help others do the same. – **Dutch Sheets**, Bestselling Author, *Intercessory Prayer*, Colorado Springs, Colorado

Endorsement: *Listen, God Is Speaking to You*

Quin Sherrer has a unique gift to present the written word in a way that allows us to know without a shadow of a doubt that if we listen, God is speaking to us. I highly recommend this deeply inspirational book to you and those you love." – **Mrs. Diana Hagee**, John Hagee Ministries, San Antonio, Texas

Endorsement: *A Mother's Guide to Praying for Your Children*

Today the Holy Spirit is preparing, training, and transforming one generation to impart the mantle of purpose to the generation that is now arising. *A Mother's Guide to Praying for Your Children* will help you draw near to God and gain revelation that will secure your inheritance for the future. Quin Sherrer will ignite your heart to pray and bring forth the redemptive purpose and success of your children. – **Chuck Pierce**, President, Global Spheres, Inc., Corinth, Texas

Endorsement: *Lord, I Need Your Healing Power: Securing God's Help in Sickness and Trials*

I was privileged to be the pastor who encouraged Quin to believe in healing and to write about it more than 30 years ago – starting with Bill Lance, whose story of healing which Quin wrote won her the Guidepost magazine writers contest. This book is packed with testimonies of those who have been touched by God's healing power. As you read it and study the Scriptures, new hope will rise in you. – **The Rev. Forrest Mobley, Ph.D.**, Immanuel Anglican Church, Destin, Florida

Books by Quin Sherrer and Ruthanne Garlock

Becoming a Spirit-Led Mom
The Beginners Guide to Receiving the Holy Spirit
God Be with Us: A Daily Guide to Praying for Our Nation (finalist for Gold Medallion Award, devotional category, 2002)
Grandma, I Need Your Prayers: Blessing Your Grandchildren Through the Power of Prayer
How to Forgive Your Children
How to Pray for Family and Friends
How to Pray for Your Children
Lord, I Need to Pray with Power
Lord, I Need Your Healing Power
The Making of a Spiritual Warrior: A Woman's Guide to Daily Victory
Prayer Partnerships: Experiencing the Power of Agreement
Prayers Women Pray: Intimate Moments with God
Praying Prodigals Home: Taking Back What the Enemy Has Stolen
The Spiritual Warrior's Prayer Guide
A Woman's Guide to Breaking Bondages
A Woman's Guide to Getting Through Tough Times
A Woman's Guide to Spirit-Filled Living
A Woman's Guide to Spiritual Warfare
You Can Break That Habit and Be Free

Books by Quin Sherrer

Good Night, Lord: Inspiration for the End of the Day
Hope for a Widow's Heart: Encouraging Reflections for Your Journey
A House of Many Blessings: The Joy of Christian Hospitality (with Laura Watson)
How to Pray for Your Children
Listen, God Is Speaking to You: True Stories of His Love and Guidance
Miracles Happen When You Pray: True Stories of the Remarkable Power of Prayer
A Mother's Guide to Praying for Your Children
Prayers from a Grandmother's Heart
The Warm and Welcome Home

Books Contributed to by Quin Sherrer

A Treasury of Prayers for Mothers
The Deborah Company
Women of Prayer: Released to the Nations

Bibles Contributed to by Quin Sherrer

The Grandmother's Bible
Women of Destiny Bible: Women Mentoring Women Through the Scriptures

APPENDIX C: NOTES

Part One: Casting a Shadow on a Mountaintop

1. Jamie Buckingham, taped message to Women's Aglow Fellowship Conference, New Orleans, LA. Fall 1987. Used with permission of Mrs. Jamie Buckingham.
2. www.cute-calendar.com/event/repentance-day/16764.html. Accessed June 23, 2016.
3. www:wgm.org/png. Accessed August 12, 2016.
4. Dutch Sheets, *Intercessory Prayer* (Ventura, CA: Regal Books, 1996), 125.
5. Veronica Zundel, *Eerdman's Book of Famous Prayers* (Grand Rapids, MI: Eerdmans, 1983), 51.
6. Adapted from Quin Sherrer, *Good Night, Lord* (Grand Rapids, MI: Chosen, a division of Baker Publishing Group, 2000), 193. Used with permission.
7. Bruce Wilkinson, *The Prayer of Jabez* (Sisters, OR: Multnomah Publishers, 2000), 41.
8. *Merriam-Webster's Learner's Dictionary.* www.learnersdictionary.com/definition/influence. Accessed September 29, 2016.
9. John C. Maxwell, *Developing the Leader Within You* (Nashville, TN: Thomas Nelson, 1993), 2.
10. Rick Warren, blog for July 16, 2014. http://pastors.com/kingdombuilders-2/. Accessed September 28, 2016.

Part Two: Connecting with Purpose and Influence

1. Wayne Cordeiro, *Doing Church as a Team* (Ventura, CA: Regal Books, 2001), 114.
2. Ibid., 114-115.
3. Rick Warren, *The Purpose Driven Life* (Grand Rapids, MI: Zondervan, 2002), 242.

4. Bruce Wilkinson, *The Prayer of Jabez* (Sisters, OR: Multnomah Publications, 2000), 40.

5. Karl A Barden, *The Activated Church* (Shippenberg, PA: Destiny Image, 1992), 92-93.

6. Rick Warren, blog for July 16, 2014, http://pastors.com/kingdom-builders-2/.

7. Terry Crist, *Awakened to Destiny* (Lake Mary, FL: Charisma House, 2002), 220.

8. Chuck Pierce, *The Best is Yet Ahead* (Colorado Springs, CO: Wagner Publication, 2001), 34.

Part Three: Mentoring One Another

1. Edgar A. Guest http://www.wow4u.com/edgar-guest/. Accessed June 28, 2016.

2. Win Couchman, quoted in Dee Brestin, *The Friendship of Women* (Wheaton, IL: Victor Books, 1989), 162.

3. "The Life of Howard G. 'Prof' Hendricks," DTS Voice, https://voice.dts.edu/article/howard-hendricks-prof/.

4. Bobb Biehl, *Mentoring: Confidence in Finding a Mentor and Becoming One* (Nashville, TN: Broadman and Holman Publishers, 1996), 60-61.

5. Howard C. Hendricks, *Seven Promises of a Promise Keeper* (Colorado Springs, CO: Focus on the Family Publishers, 1994), 42-48.

6. Bobb Biehl, *Mentoring: Confidence in Finding a Mentor and Becoming One* (Nashville, TN: Broadman and Holman Publishers, 1996), 179.

7. Joel Osteen, *I Declare: 31 Promises to Speak over Your Life* (New York, NY: Faith Works, 2012), 19.

8. Gigi Tchividjian-Graham, *Passing It On* (New York, NY: McCracken Press, 1993), 14.

9. Bobby Conner, "Should I Concern Myself with the Legacy I Leave Behind? A Good Man Leaves an Inheritance." *The Elijah List*. Internet accessed July 31, 2014.

10. *Masterpieces of Religious Verses*, ed. James Dalton Morrison (New York, NY: Harper and Row, 1948), 389.

11. Dana Perino, *And the Good News Is…Lessons and Advice from the Bright Side* (New York, NY: Twelve Hachette Book Group, 2015), 160.

12. Other mentoring programs are listed online, designed to answer specific questions and to fit busy schedules. But be aware that many have varying fees for lessons or videos.

13. John Maxwell, *Developing the Leaders Around You* (Nashville, TN: Thomas Nelson Publishers, copyright by Injoy, Inc., 1995), 97.

14. Baukje Doormenbal, *Homemaking* (Colorado Springs, CO: NavPress, 1981), 4.

15. Quin Sherrer, *The Warm and Welcome Home* (Ventura, CA: Regal, 2002), 107-108.

16. Diane Lake, *Elijah List*, www:elijahlist.com, Diane Lake website: www:starfireministries.org. Accessed February 15, 2016.

17. Quin Sherrer and Ruthanne Garlock, *A Woman's Guide to Spirit Filled Living* (Ann Arbor, MI: Servant Publication, 1996), 98-99.

Part Four: Encouraging One Another

1. Fred Roberts, *The World According to Mister Rogers: Important Things to Remember* (New York, NY: Hyperion Books, Family Communications, Inc., 2003), 78.

2. Quin Sherrer, *Good Night, Lord* (Grand Rapids, MI: Chosen, a division of Baker Publishing Group), 2000), 91. Used with permission.

Part Five: Contributing to Needs of Others

1. Bruce Wilkinson, *The Prayer of Jabez* (Sisters, OR: Multnomah Publishers, 2000), 39-40.

2. Excerpted from *Listen, God is Speaking to You*, Quin Sherrer (Ann Arbor, MI: Servant Publication, 1999), 174-175.

3. Wayne Cordeiro, *Doing Church as a Team* (Ventura, CA: Regal Books, 2001), 100.

4. Kathy Deering, *Gifted for Good* (Ann Arbor, MI: Servant Publication, 2000), 69-70.

5. (Quoting the mother, Kari Duane) AP story quoted KCRA-TV and BuzzFeed in article; Accessed October 19, 2015. http://foxnews.com/us/2015/10/19cancelled-california-wedding.

Part Six: Praying for One Another

1. Quin Sherrer, *Listen, God Is Speaking to You* (Ann Arbor, MI: Servant Publications, 1999), 189-190.
2. Dutch Sheets, *Intercessory Prayer* (Ventura, CA: Regal, 1996), 45.
3. Quin Sherrer, *Good Night, Lord* (Grand Rapids, MI: Chosen, a division of Baker Publishing Group, 2000), 18. Used with permission.
4. Elizabeth George, *Life Management for Busy Women* (Eugene, OR: Harvest House Publishers, 2002), 99.
5. Quin Sherrer, *A Mother's Guide to Praying for Your Children* (Grand Rapids, MI: Chosen Books, a division of Baker Publishing Group, 2010) 39, 127-129.
6. Quin Sherrer and Ruthanne Garlock, *Lord, I Need to Pray With Power* (Lake Mary, FL: Charisma House, 2007), 121.
7. James W. Goll, *The Lost Art of Intercession* (Shippenburg, PA: Destiny Image, 1997), 77-78.
8. James W. Goll. Ibid. 78.
9. Internet: http://www.spiritus-temporis.com/john-wesley/moravian-influence.html. Accessed July 4, 2016.
10. James W. Goll, *The Lost Art of Intercession* (Shippenburg, PA: Destiny Image, 1997), 99.
11. Dutch Sheets, *Intercessory Prayer* (Ventura, CA: Regal Publishing, 1996), 155.
12. Alvin VanderGriend, *Intercessors for America Newsletter*, March 1999. (See Houses of Prayer Everywhere, HOPE website.)
13. Quin Sherrer and Ruthanne Garlock, *A Woman's Guide to Spiritual Warfare, Revised Edition* (Grand Rapids, MI: Chosen Books, a division of Baker Publishing Group, 2017), 223-225.

Part Seven: Serving One Another

1. Janet and Geoff Benge, *Something Greater than Gold* (Seattle, WA: Youth With a Mission Publishers), 1998.
2. Mike Huckabee, *Do the Right Thing* (New York, NY: The Penguin Group USA, 2008), 192.
3. B. H. Powers, *The Henrietta Mears Story* (Westwood, NJ: Fleming H. Revell Company, 1957).

4. Helen Kooiman Hosier, *100 Christian Women Who Changed the 20th Century* (Grand Rapids, MI: Revell, 2000), 170-176.

5. E. O. Roe, Ed. *Dream Big: The Henrietta Mears Story* (Ventura, CA: Regal Books, 1990).

6. Hosier, *100 Christian Women Who Changed the 20th Century.* Ibid. 173.

7. After many decades, Gospel Light is no longer publishing. Books that Quin Sherrer wrote for Gospel Light are now available through Chosen, a division of Baker Publishing Group, Grand Rapids, MI. Phone 616-676-9573.

8. Dr. Frank Laubach, www.hermes-press.com/laubach2.htm). Accessed February 24, 2016.

9. Ibid.

Part Eight: Laying Down Your Life for One Another

1. Ed Vulliamy, *War on Terrorism: Observer Special*, Ed Vulliamy in New York, Saturday, December 1, 2001. Last modified on Monday, January 18, 2016.

2. "The Story of Flight 93," Dateline NBC, aired Oct. 2, 2001. Interview by Stone Phillips.

3. Ed Vulliamy, *War on Terrorism*: Ibid.

4. Lisa Beamer with Ken Abraham, *Let's Roll* (Wheaton, IL: Tyndale House Publishers, Inc., 2002), 31-32.

5. Ibid. 107.

6. Ibid. 301, 296.

7. Ibid. 303.

8. CNN.com./U.S. "Transcript of Bush speech in Atlanta" posted November 8, 2001. Accessed Internet, September 12, 2017.

9. The Rev. Norvel Goff. http://www.daily mail.co.uk/news/article-3134119/Thousands-march-Charleston-bridge.

10. Ibid.

11. Ibid.

12. Clement of Alexander, *Topical Encyclopedia of Living Quotations* (Minneapolis, MN: Bethany House Publishers, 1982), 10.

13. Faith Karimi, CNN, filed Aug 23 and updated September 5, 2015, http//www.wptv.co,/news/world/alex-skarlatos-anthony-sandler.

14. "Mysterious Ways," Guideposts Publication (New York, NY: December-January 2016), 4.
15. Gracia Burnham with Dean Merrill, *To Fly Again* (Wheaton, IL: Tyndale House Publishers, 2005), 12. Also see *In the Presence of My Enemies* by same authors.

Part Nine: Caring for One Another – Friendships

1. Graham Cooke, *God's Keeping Power* (Kent, England: Sovereign World International, 2004), 55.
2. Graham Cooke, Ibid., 38-39.
3. James H. Strong, *Strong's Exhaustive Concordance, Old Testament*, #8104.
4. Graham Cooke, Ibid., 55.
5. Charles R. Swindoll, *Simple Faith* (Dallas, TX: Word Publishing, 1991), 111.
6. "Why Men Are Bad at Friendships" by Daniel Duane, quoting the Male Deficit Model http://www.huffington-post.com/2014/07/15/men-and-friendship_n_557578.html. Accessed, July 23, 2016.

Part Ten: Influencing from Things Other than People

1. Franklin Graham, *Rebel Without a Cause* (Nashville, TN: Thomas Nelson, 1995), 314.
2. http://blogs.bible.org/engage/gail_seidel/learning_from_brother_lawrence_-_a_simple_17th_century_monk and https://en.wikipedia.org/wiki/Brother_Lawrence.
3. Ibid.
4. www.utmost.org/oswald-chambers-bio/. Taken from *The Quotable Oswald Chambers*.
5. Oswald Chambers, *My Utmost for His Highest*, https://www.goodreads.com/work/quotes/1559310-my-utmost-for-his-highest.
6. michellevle.com/2015/01/23wrote-utmost-highest-part-11.
7. WholesomeWords.org from Profiles in Evangelism by Fred Barlow, Sword of the Lord Publishers, ©1976, 2015.
8. Sam Wellman, *William Carey, Father of Modern Missions* (Uhrichville, OH: Barbour Publishing, 1997).

9. WholesomeWords.org from Profiles in Evangelism by Fred Barlow, Sword of the Lord Publishers, ©1976, 2015.

10. https://www.goodreads.com/author/quotes/396826.William _Carey.

Part Eleven: Leaving a Legacy in Others

1. John Maxwell, *The Maxwell Daily Devotion* (Nashville, TN: Thomas Nelson 2007), 397.

2. Vocabulary.com.Dictionary. Accessed May 1, 2017.

3. https://www.goodreads.com/quotes/1754593-an-inheritance-is-what-you-leave-with-people-a-legacy.

4. Quin Sherrer, *Good Night, Lord* (Ventura, CA: Regal Books, 2000), 232.

5. Jack Hayford, ed. *New Spirit-Filled Life Bible* (Nashville, TN: Thomas Nelson), 1564.

6. Jamie Buckingham, "Dreaming the Impossible Dream," article, *Logos Journal* (Plainfield, NJ: January-February, 1975), 23.

7. Jane Kilpatrick, *Every Fixed Star* (Colorado Springs, CO: Waterbrook Press, 2012), 6.

8. Edwards, http://self-discipline.8m.com/generational-discipline.htm. by Michael Janke, Discipline article, accessed July 10, 2016; article by William P Farley. Accessed September 2, 2016. http://enrichmentjournal.ag.org/20(0201/200201_104_johnathan.cfm. (Note: He says Edwards only had 11 children.)

9. Terry Christ, *Awakened to Destiny* (Lake Mary, FL: Christmas House, 2002).

10. Eddie Snipes, *Exchanged Life Outreach* "Three Principles of Discipleship (Part 2)." www.exchangedlife.com/sermon/topical/discip-2_2.html.

11. Gail Schoettler, former Lt. Governor and Treasurer of Colorado in a newspaper column in the Denver Post, 2001, saying she borrowed the quiz.

Part Twelve: Remembering the Past

1. Apollo 13 Quotes, 1995, http://www.imdb.com/title/tt0112384/quotes. Accessed December 13, 2017.

2. William Penn: http://www.quotegarden.com/helping.html. Accessed April 7, 2017.

3. Quin Sherrer, *Good Night, Lord* (Ventura, CA: Regal Books, 2000), 219-220.

4. Robert Burns, Poem, "Prayer in the Prospect of Death" http://www.bbc.co.uk/arts/robertburns/works/a_prayer in_ the_prospect_of_death/. Accessed July 15, 2017.

5. http://www.cityofliterature.com/a-to-z/writers-museum-2/. Accessed March 22, 2017.

6. https://en.wikipedia.org/wiki/Robert_Louis_Stevenson. Accessed March 22, 2017.

7. August 1, 2011 by Carltown 17 Comments. (Footnote: Begin the Adventure by Carl Townsent in Creatingnew-worlds.org.what-did-the-queen-of Scotland fear. Accessed March 22, 2017.

8. Arthur Fawcett, *The Cambuslang Revival: The Scottish Evangelical Revival of the Eighteenth Century* (Carlisle, PA: The Banner of Truth Trust Publishers, 1971) 64.

9. Francis Scott Key, Written During War of 1812 when Britain was shelling U.S. ships; from fourth verse. Adopted by Congress as U.S. National Anthem in 1931.

10. https:/www.britannica.com/event/Bataan-Death-March by Elizabeth M. Norman. Accessed January 25, 2018.

11. Kenneth W. Osbeck, *101 More Hymn Stories* (Grand Rapids, MI: Kregel Publishing, 1985), 34-35.

12. Quin Sherrer and Ruthanne Garlock, *Lord, I Need to Pray With Power* (Lake Mary, FL: Charisma House, 2007), 98.

Part Thirteen: Coming Full Circle

1. John Maxwell, *Be All You Can Be* (Colorado Springs, CO: Victor, a division of Cook Publishing, 2002, originally 1987), 29.

2. Excerpted from Quin Sherrer, *Good Night, Lord* (Ventura, CA: Regal Books, 2002), 241.

3. Jamie Buckingham, "Dreaming the Impossible Dream" (Plainfield, NJ: Logos Journal, January-February,1972), 26.

4. Dutch Sheets, *Dream: Discovering God's Purpose for Your Life* (Minneapolis, MI: Bethany House, 2012), 11-12.

5. Quin Sherrer, *Hope for a Widow's Heart: Encouraging Reflections for Your Journey* (Franklin, TN: Authentic Publications, 2013), 3-4.

6. Linda Ellis, www.lindaellis.net/the dash.

7. Dolores Meritt, Obituary, *Northwest Florida Daily News*, Ft. Walton Beach, FL: April 19, 2008.

8. Jamie Buckingham, *The Nazarene: Intimate Insights into the Savior's Life* (Ann Arbor, MI: Servant Publication, 1991), 89.

9. Buckingham, Ibid. 89.

Appendix A

1. Quin Sherrer, *A Mother's Guide to Praying for Your Children* (Grand Rapids, MI: Chosen, a division of Baker Book Publishing, 2011), 135-136.

ABOUT THE AUTHOR

Quin Sherrer has written or co-authored 30 books (primarily with Ruthanne Garlock) including bestsellers *A Woman's Guide to Spiritual Warfare*, *Miracles Happen When You Pray*, and *How to Pray for Your Children*. Their devotional book *God Be with Us: A Daily Guide to Praying for Our Nation* was a Gold Medallion Awards finalist, given by the Evangelical Christian Publishers Association. Crossings and Guideposts Book Clubs have also published her titles.

Quin's book sales have exceeded a million copies, not counting those translated into other languages. She has spoken to audiences in 47 States and 12 nations, encouraging them in their daily, and sometimes challenging, walks of faith. She's addressed topics of prayer, hospitality, miracles, and personal renewal as a guest on more than 350 radio and television programs – including The 700 Club, 100 Huntley Street, Daystar Television Network, and the Trinity Broadcasting Network.

Quin holds a B.S. degree in journalism from Florida State University. She spent her early career writing for newspapers and magazines in the Cape Kennedy, Florida area where her late husband LeRoy was a NASA engineer. A winner of Guideposts magazine's writing contest, she also was named Writer of the Year at the Florida Writers in Touch Conference.

She served on Aglow International board of directors for some years. Quin often speaks to church groups, weekend seminars, Sunday congregations, professional groups, and on U.S. military bases. She has three children and six grandchildren.

She may be contacted on her website: www.quinsherrer.com.

Made in the USA
Columbia, SC
21 August 2019